The

MESSY NARROW ROAD

The

MESSY NARROW ROAD

A Fellow Traveler's Tips and Encouragement

Vicky J. Wedel

Published by Redemption Press, PO Box 427, Enumclaw, WA 98022.
Toll-Free (844) 2REDEEM (273-3336)

Redemption Press is honored to present this title in partnership with the author. The views expressed or implied in this work are those of the author. Redemption Press provides our imprint seal representing design excellence, creative content, and high quality production.

ISBN 13: 978-1-64645-490-7 (Paperback)
978-1-64645-488-4 (ePub)
978-1-64645-489-1 (Mobi)

LCCN 2021915497

Contents

Acknowledgments

Special thanks to everyone
who encouraged me
to publish this book.

To my friends, Joni and Jennifer,
for reviewing this book
and making suggestions.
They were greatly needed.

Deepest gratitude to my friend, Kelley,
for being the hands and feet of Christ
during my every trial.

Introduction

This book wasn't planned, that is, by me. I believe it is a gift from God. How can I make such a bold statement? Before 2017, I didn't write devotions or poems. I'm not a big reader and would never choose a book of poetry because I have found most of them dark or confusing. But one day God started laying words on my heart. So I began writing poems; then later, devotions.

After being encouraged to write a book, my friend Joni suggested I pair each devotion with a poem. As each devotion was written (with the exception of one), I found God had already given me the poem much earlier. Please don't misunderstand, the book you hold is not God's infallible Word (the Bible), though it includes many Bible verses.

We live in a broken and fallen world. Much prayer went into the process as my friend helped me compile which devotions and poems would be included. The writing has been worship for me because I'm sharing truths God has taught me through both studying the Bible and living the painful consequences brought on by decisions I and others have made. With each trial, I've seen God continue to prove Himself to be all He claims to be. The darker the situation, the brighter He shines through it.

Words are powerful and I've grown a love for them. Words, though, can mean different things to different people. Words like faith, God, truth, and belief have different definitions depending on a person's worldview. Therefore, I feel it's necessary to clarify the words *us* and *we* and phrases such as *His own* used in this book.

These words refer to believers in Christ, those who believe Jesus, the one and only Son of God, died on the cross to take the punishment our wrongs deserve and rose from the dead to prove it (1 Cor. 15:3–4). God's promises are as true today as they were when first spoken and penned. His promises are for all who are willing to accept His Son as their personal Savior and Lord over their lives. If you don't know God like this, turn the page to discover who He is. Better yet, open His infallible Word, the Bible. God wants you to accept all He is so He can give you all He promises.

If you're a brother or sister in Christ, hello, forever family. My hope is that you too find yourself worshiping the One who loves us more than we can fathom. How I long for the day when we're in heaven, worshiping the Lamb fully as He deserves.

If this book finds you in the middle of a trial, take heart. We're one day closer to seeing Christ face to face! Until then, let's trust Him and seek His guidance. Let's purpose to set our faces like flint as our Savior did when He rose from His knees after praying in the garden. When we feel hopeless, like those at the foot of the cross who didn't understand why Christ was being crucified, let's remember all that came from the darkest day in history. Let's allow our trials to refine us so we better reflect our Savior. May each trial teach us more about ourselves and how much we need our Savior every day. As we cling to Him, He'll lift our gaze away from the cares of this world and to His fullness.

You're not alone on your journey. He is near and you have a forever family also walking the messy road. Maybe one way we will spend eternity is by sharing the stories of how He carried us through. If so, I sure look forward to hearing yours.

Take heart, precious family, we're one day closer!

—Vicky

The Messy Narrow Road

The only way to reside in heaven isn't by being good or just wanting to,
God tells us in Scripture[1] we're sinners and at death our payment is due.
By nature we aren't born seeing rightly, blinded to the ways of God,
Our wrongdoings seem right to us, only proving our thinking flawed.
But since God is the perfect Creator, He, not man, sets the rules,
We can accept God's way to heaven, or defy Him, dying as fools.

To believe takes complete acceptance that all God says is true,
His perfect Son died to pay our debt and was raised to life anew.
With confession of Jesus as Lord, we're placed on the Narrow Road,
To live differently than unbelievers, those still "kicking against the goad." [2]
It takes Christ's work for salvation, and God's power to live differently,
God makes way for His children to seek guidance expectantly.

The Road requires humility and surrendering to the Father's way,
Trusting as Jesus did on earth, depending on His Father every day.
He is our hope in every situation, delighting in Him helps us be still,
Bringing our heart and arms wide open, like Christ on Calvary's hill.
The Narrow Road can look messy from a traveler's point of view,
Living for the Father guarantees we'll reach heaven black and blue.

Sometimes our wounds are self-inflicted, because we've chosen to sin,
With repentance, the Father lifts us up, dusting off to begin again.
Bumps and bruises we'll have plenty, but healing gives the chance,
For God's power to be put on display, giving others of Him a glance.
Do you trust in Jesus' death? If so, you too are on the Narrow Road.
Let's take the yoke He's offered, so the Savior can lighten our load.

---

[1] The Bible, the Word of God.
[2] Acts 26:13–18, the words of Jesus to Paul who was defying Him as the Messiah God sent.

But small is the gate and narrow the road that leads to life, and only a few find it.
—Matthew 7:14

Jesus answered, "I am the way and the truth and the life. No one comes to the Father except through me."
—John 14:6

But God demonstrated his own love for us in this: While we were still sinners, Christ died for us.
—Romans 5:8

Take my yoke upon you and learn from me, for I am gentle and humble in heart, and you will find rest for your souls. For my yoke is easy and my burden is light.
—Matthew 11:29-30

ONE

Always Extreme

*W*e live in a world of extremes and can easily think in words of extremes: all or nothing, always or never. These words are rarely the case of whatever or whomever we're talking about. If we say, "He always does that," it would be wise to pause and consider, does he really do that at all times?

We use extremes to make a point. We use extremes to express strong feelings we have about a situation or person. But extremes require perfect consistency to be fulfilled, and no one is perfectly consistent but God. Even the most faithful friend will let us down. Even the most careless people will do something considerate. They may do it for selfish reasons, but they still do things that benefit others.

God is like no other (Isa. 45:5). He is other than anyone or anything. God is always perfect (Ps. 18:30). God never changes (Mal. 3:6). If God could change, He'd be less than Himself making Him no longer perfect. He will never lie because He can't (1 Sam. 15:29). So when He says He is faithful (1 Cor. 1:9), He is. He always will be and will never be unfaithful.

We have an extreme God! When He uses extreme words in Scripture, we can bank on them! When we praise Him for who He is or speak of His character to another, we can use extreme words liberally because they are always true. But when we praise Him or speak of His character, do we believe what we're saying, I mean really believe?

Meditating on His extremely good character also helps us to see our lack of it. This isn't to shame us but to lead us to extreme gratitude that He is not like us. Yet still, He has chosen us to be His own. We can change from being devoted followers to little rebels in a millisecond, but He never lessens His devotion to us (Jer. 31). We fail Him but He never fails us (Ps. 73:26). God has grafted us into His forever family through Jesus and will never cut us off (Eph. 2:12–13). We may forget to whom we belong, but He never forgets us (Isa. 49:15)!

When life seems extremely hard, match it with God's extreme character.

If you think you'll never find peace in a relationship, remember the One you've been given forever peace with through the blood of His Son (Phil. 4:9).

If you feel hopeless in a situation, remember the hope you have in Him, and that His hope will never disappoint (Rom. 5:5).

Whatever the struggle, match it with God's character and feel the struggle lose its power. The more this is done, the less often you will use extreme words on those who aren't.

We'll never grasp the depth of God's extremeness, even in heaven. But the more we try, the more often we'll find ourselves overwhelmed by Him.

> Oh, the depths of the riches both of the wisdom and knowledge of God! "How unsearchable his judgments and his paths beyond tracing out!" "Who has known the mind of the Lord? Or who has been his counselor?" "Who has ever given to God that God should repay him?" For from him and through him and to him are all things. To him be the glory forever! Amen.
> —Romans 11:33-36

Who God Is

Transcendent like no other, God cannot be compared,
Needs nothing, stands alone, His essence isn't shared.
Creator, Sustainer, Provider, nothing does He lack,
His power makes demons shudder and men draw back.

Immutable perfection, no changes could improve,
Always just in His justice, no sin does He approve.
Giving every man a conscience, no one has excuse,
Offers all salvation, but the "wise" find it abstruse.

Rightly He judges, and the repentant He forgives,
Extravagant Father, to the generous He outgives.
He sets the standard, only able to do good,
Redeems His own while sinners, in their place He stood.

Longsuffering in the waiting for all to be made right,
Gives the faint of heart who ask endurance and might.
Timekeeper and Time Maker, but never in a hurry,
Trustworthy and dependable, nothing makes Him worry.

Holds all things together, and holds tightly to His own,
No need to fear, He's in control, and still upon His throne.
Constantly working all for good, no pain goes to waste,
None compares to the banqueting table His own will taste.

He provides the courage in those who on Him meditate,
Transfixed by His character, feel fear and worry evaporate.
Each trait to the fullest and extreme, impossible to add,
Incomprehensible yet knowable, to those who call Him "Dad."

> For you did not receive a spirit that makes
> you a slave again to fear, but you received
> the Spirit of sonship. And by him we cry,
> "Abba, Father."
>
> —Romans 8:15

When do I use extreme statements?

What extreme character of God do I need to meditate upon?

Two

What Are You Worth?

The world rates worth by physical or mental characteristics. Value might be determined by income or benefit one brings to the home, workplace, relationship, or society. It's difficult to see how wrong the world's perspective is because we're continually fed this erroneous point of view. Within such a cold-hearted culture, no wonder people struggle to feel valued. We crave feeling we have worth. If value and worth are felt, it often comes with a side of fear. The fear of losing the "value" we worked so hard to obtain.

Believers have an opportunity to know their worth with no fear attached. It's simple but not easy, and it takes time and effort.

There is no better way to right a flawed perspective than to look through the lens of the cross. God made clear our real value through the cost His Son paid (Rom. 6:23). The more we know of Jesus, the more we comprehend His worthiness—and the worth God has placed on us.

Don't feel worthy? We shouldn't. If we do, we're still stuck in the world's perspective.

God's Word transforms the way we see ourselves. But because we're bent to the world's way, we struggle and default back to our old way of thinking.

Here is where the effort comes in: it takes intentional effort to spend time in the Bible each day, pray, and be with those who do the same. God is faithful, and over time, through His Word and His people, He'll continually reveal the lies of the world. Time in truth also deepens an awareness of the price that was paid on our behalf.

The world's perspective feeds us hatred of self (shame) or pride because man believes worth comes from what we do. Unfortunately, we can't do enough to make up for our wrongs, and we can't make ourselves better (Rom. 3:10–20).

But what we can do is learn the heart of God and accept ourselves as He does. He knows us fully (warts and all), values us completely (not based on what we do), and loves us more than we can ever imagine, as Jesus fully displayed on the cross.

To see things properly, we must feed upon God's perfect perspective found in the Bible. Need to right your perspective? Go to the source—the One who can be trusted to set it straight.

O, LORD, you have searched me and you know me. You know when I sit and when I rise; you perceive my thoughts from afar. You discern my going out and my lying down; you are familiar with all my ways. Before a word is on my tongue you know it completely, O LORD. You hem me in behind and before; you have laid your hand upon me. Such knowledge is too wonderful for me, too lofty for me to attain. Where can I go from your Spirit? Where can I flee from your presence? If I go up to the heavens, you are there; if I make my bed in the depths, you are there. If I rise on the wings of the dawn, if I settle on the far side of the sea, even there your hand will guide me, your right hand will hold me fast.
—Psalm 139:1-10

But when the time had fully come, God sent his Son, born of a woman, born under law, to redeem those under law, that we might receive the full rights of sons. Because you are sons, God sent the Spirit of his Son into our hearts, the Spirit who calls out, "Abba, Father." So you are no longer a slave, but a son; and since you are a son, God has made you also an heir.
—Galatians 4:4-7

For Christ died for sins once for all, the righteous for the unrighteous, to bring you to God.
—1 Peter 3:18

Source of Worth and Value

The Liar's constantly saying, "Your value's set by what you do,
You're only valuable if productive," even though that's not true.
"Your value must be proven, you're not enough, make up by work.
To live worn out is beneficial, resting is shameful, so don't shirk."

"Hurry, hurry, you're running late, you'll never get it all done.
You have no time to pray or read, no time to spend with that Son.
God understands you're busy, no need to listen to that small voice.
You've got too much to do. God understands you have no choice."

"You're not good enough, try harder, you can't afford to fail again.
It's every man for himself, don't ask for help, other's loss is your win.
Stay busy in mind and body, being still means you're getting behind.
Keep working to have more than enough, that's how success is defined."

Does the Enemy have you fooled? Have his lies been heard and believed?
Are you busy chasing your tail to be valued, forgetting it's been received?
You've been created in God's image, your value and worth already given,
God proved it by giving His Son to die; trusting this means you're forgiven.

God knows you have much to do, He holds your present and future secure,
Satan knows spending time in prayer and the Bible transforms to endure.
God's full of grace and mercy, He understands how hard this world is,
Having lived in the flesh, He was tempted, and died to make you His.

Mistakes you'll make, but remember each "failure" provides feedback,
Ask God for the way of escape when Satan, the world, or flesh attack.
Whatever you do, do for Jesus, trusting Him with what's undone,
Nothing changes how He sees you, His own He'll never shun.

Begin each day with truth, recalibrate your mind to the Source,
He set your worth in blood, and sealed with the Spirit to endorse.
Let all work become worship, and you'll find joy even in menial tasks,
With your self-worth secure, excitement grows to do whatever God asks.

But now, this is what the LORD says he who created you, O Jacob, he who formed you, O Israel: "Fear not, for I have redeemed you; I have summoned you by name; you are mine."
—Isaiah 43:1

For it is by grace you have been saved, through faith and this not from yourselves, it is the gift of God not by works, so that no one can boast.
—Ephesians 2:8-9

How do I define my worth?

What lies have I believed, and how do they contradict God's Word?

THREE

Lift the Veil

What gifts God has given His own! One of these gifts is not being allowed to see the depth of our own depravity. Another gift is not being allowed to see God in His fullness.

It's recorded in Exodus 33:20 that no man can see God's face and live. It seems likely the full view of our depravity would do the same—destroy us. With faith in Christ for salvation comes His gift of the Spirit to indwell us. When the Spirit came, did He bring a veil to cover the spiritual eyes we've been given? These eyes had empowered us to believe Jesus is who He claims and we deserve the punishment He took for our wrongs done. Whether there's a veil or not, praise God we can't see all He sees! In His amazing grace and mercy, He limits us from seeing what we are not yet ready to see.

Years ago, a Bible teacher taught me God is holy, like no other. I began to ask God what His holiness looks like. Then later I asked God to show me His holiness. It never dawned on me how He'd answer that prayer.

He began to show me more of my depravity. He began to give me a better perspective of how He sees my pride. He began to reveal my prideful thoughts and show me actions built by pride. I thank God that He's gentle because it hurt! This answer to prayer came at a cost of my pride. Christ already paid the penalty for my pride, turning the hurt I felt into a deeper sense of gratitude for Him. He'd hung alone for me, died my death for me, and rose from the dead to prove He'd fulfilled His promise.

God is a gentleman. He only works in us when we're willing to let Him. As He "lifts the veil" a little more, He shows us the collateral damage our sins bring to us and those around us. The reveal is painful, but for a purpose. God will use the grief and pain to grow a hatred in us for what is not of Him. He can then grow holiness in us as He is holy; that is, to live set apart from the ways of this world. His holiness is the light that shines to expose more of us. It illuminates the parts of us that need to go, which frees us to live more like Christ. There is none like Him, yet He empowers us to become more like Him. This is the beautiful, yet messy and difficult, work of sanctification.

> I gain understanding from your precepts; therefore I hate every wrong path.
> —Psalm 119:104
>
> Now we see but a poor reflection as in a mirror; then we shall see face to face. Now I know in part; then I shall know fully, even as I am fully known.
> —1 Corinthians 13:12
>
> But just as he who called you is holy, so be holy in all you do; for it is written: "Be holy because I am holy."
> —1 Peter 1:16

Only Partial View

May I see only partial view,
Some of me and some of You.
If all of me were fully shown,
All my sins to me be known,
Completely undone would I be,
Even saved, too much for me

May I see only partial view,
Some of me and some of You.
If all of You were fully shown,
All Your holiness to me known,
Too overwhelmed would I be,
Face down, too much for me.

May I see only partial view,
Some of me and some of You.
Showing me what to change,
Hiding some for now to remain.
All-consuming would it be
To see every fault in me.

May I see only partial view,
Some of me and some of You.
Only good to come I'd want to see,
For trials to come would feed anxiety.
What good You have planned for me,
To see it all I couldn't breathe.

May I see only partial view,
Some of me and some of You.
Partial view of heaven's throne,
What to others You have shown
Those in Scripture Old and New,
Just a glimpse, a partial view.

May I see only partial view,
Until in heaven I'm with You.
Only then can I take all in,
All Your glory, all my sin.
Robed in Christ's righteousness alone,
Gratefully kneeling at Your throne.

What is God revealing to me about myself?

What is God revealing to me about Himself?

Four

What Is Truth

What is truth? How would you define it? Even that question invites opinion. Opinion is what truth has become in today's world. When discussing what we believe some say, "You have your truth and I have mine."

Those who say this don't understand truth doesn't change. Truth is what is. It's fact. It doesn't require verification and validation in order to exist. It has existed way before any of us. Truth isn't subjective. It's the same for all, the homeless, the wealthy, the old, the young, the educated, and the illiterate. Truth can't be modified or watered down. When it is, it ceases to be truth. Truth is unwavering and unyielding. It is like gravity. You can believe in it or not, but it still is what it is. It can't be denied, defied, or ignored; it has the last word.

In John 18:37, Jesus stands before Pilate and says, "I am a king. In fact, for this reason I was born, and for this reason I came into the world, to testify to the truth. Everyone on the side of truth listens to me."

Pilate responded, "What is truth?" But Pilate wasn't asking Jesus. He didn't care what Jesus had to say. Pilate had the Way, the Truth, and the Life standing before him and he walked away. We, like Pilate, can be determined to stick to our way of thinking, and how we want things to be. What does this get us? A greater fall and devastation when reality smacks us in the face.

Our lives reflect what we believe to be true. We prove we believe in gravity by the decisions we make. Truth like gravity, if believed, grounds us. Those who believe and depend on truth live more emotionally stable lives.

To discover truth, we must seek it without agenda or limitations. Those who seek, find it, because God is faithful. He brings it to the ready and willing.

Sometimes truth hurts. It's hard to hear, but when accepted, transformation can begin. When we're ready to put our desires aside and trust His, we're given what we desire most—truth.

God's truth may seem to be hard to find in this world, but it's at our fingertips. All it takes is picking up the Bible or opening a Bible app. God's version of truth is the only one that is true.

The One who began all things, spoke all nature into existence, and formed us in our mother's womb is truth. He cannot lie. He only speaks truth. This makes Him all He claims to be. We can build our lives on Him.

Truth sets us free—free from our wrong way of thinking, free from lies we've been told and tell ourselves. The more we accept what God says is, the more we'll desire only to live by truth. Living in truth is the safest place to dwell.

Guide me in your truth and teach me, for you are God my Savior, and my hope is in you all day long.
—Psalm 25:5

Then you will know the truth, and the truth will set you free.
—John 8:32

Jesus answered, "I am the way and the truth and the life. No one comes to the Father except through me."
—John 14:6

Words of Life

No one can ever silence Jesus the King,
The Word made flesh, on Him believers cling.
Though over and over again, many have tried,
Martyring believers, those whom in Christ abide.
Killing God's messengers won't ever affect,
The words of truth go on, even if some reject.
No matter what those refusing truth through time try to do,
No one can silence the One forever called Faithful and True.

They tried to mute Jesus, crying, "Crucify,"
To win the crowd over, the leaders had to lie.
Choosing not Jesus, but Barabbas instead,
Releasing an evil one, they'd soon again dread.
Jews, Romans, and Gentiles, those religious and not,
Each had played a part, but God wrote the plot.
Attempting to stay in power, hoping they'd still rule,
True power never theirs, they acted the fool.

Not seeking truth still occurs, both then and today,
Rejecting the Christ, the Truth, the Life, and the Way.
Those who refuse Jesus, refuse to accept His Word,
Are blind to truth before them, and deaf when it is heard.
Refusing God's only Son, all Jesus claims to be,
Rejects the Savior and His work on Calvary.
Unbelievers want to silence God's truth for good,
Unwilling to accept, but no one ever could.

For God is Creator and sovereign over all,
Even those who respond to truth with appall.
His truth can't be silenced, paused, or muted,
Truth is what is, whether denied or refuted.
One day all will see truth for what and who it is,
Not truth according to man's definition, but His.
Whoever asks, "What is truth?" with humility,
Finds faith and words of life given generously.

Then Jesus cried out, "When a man believes in me, he doesn't believe in me only, but in the one who sent me."
—John 12:44

Sanctify them in the truth; your word is truth.
—John 17:17

What truth of God am I struggling to accept?

How do I respond when someone refuses the truth?

FIVE

His Children

How is spiritual maturity measured? Not by the length of time we've been believers, nor by our amount of biblical knowledge. This is the world's way of measuring, not God's (1 Sam. 16:7). These alone can only grow pride not maturity. Spiritual maturity takes time and truth.

Maturity takes the mindset of a child. The young are dependent; the younger they are the more helpless. This mindset is how we came to faith. We needed God to do what only He can do, make us right with Himself (John 3:18; 14:6).

Jesus illustrated this when He was speaking and some listening began to bring their children to Him. The apostles rebuked them, but Jesus called the children to Himself saying, "Let the little children come to me, and do not hinder them, for the kingdom of God belongs to such as these" (Luke 18:16). "Such as these" means the children, the helpless, and emptyhanded. This is how we come to faith, emptyhanded and willing to receive what God provides.

With faith, we're given a Helper (John 16:5–15). With faith, we're made more than conquerors (Rom. 8:31–39). With faith, we can do all things (find contentment no matter our circumstances) through Christ who gives us strength (Phil. 4:13). These are just a few of the incredible promises we receive.

We can get caught up in all we receive, forgetting we came helpless. Our sin nature (our flesh) still remains. It's still alive and kicking, just ask those who live with you. Our pride leads us to think we're no longer helpless, or weak and needy, but we are. Being saved doesn't mean we're fully sanctified—that comes in heaven. Until then, in us—that is our nature—there is still no good found (Rom. 7:18). We still require God for everything good. Only He can grow and empower us to live as He has called us to live (James 4; 1 Pet. 4).

The more we grasp our helplessness, the more we'll see ourselves as we are—His children. Accepting our helplessness is hard because it goes against our nature, but it is the best place to be. Acceptance brings peace knowing we're in the hands of our Provider. It brings a willingness to ask Him for and receive the help we need. A friend of mine said it well when describing our relationship with God, "We bring our sin, and God brings everything else."

Since we're God's children, it would serve us well to spend time with Him and share with Him how we really feel. We can go to Him squealing with delight and tell Him how grateful we are. We can also run to Him with disappointments and tears because we need His comfort and healing. All our feelings are safe with Him. He already knows them, but often we don't until we start praying.

The more we talk to Him and spend time with Him as His children, the more we'll be full of wonder when looking at nature and captivated by Him because of the unfathomable details of His creation (Rom. 1:20). Living as His children is freeing and fun! It's safe to make mistakes because He expects them. When our world turns upside down, we know where to run. No wonder Jesus said the kingdom of God is such as these!

Like a Child

Christ Jesus came in the flesh for everyone to see,
He is God's only Son, Lord of you and me.
He came for all, the young, old, big, and small,
There is no limit to whom the Master will call.

When on earth, the disciples held off the little ones,
Jesus rebuked them saying, "Let the children come."
Sometimes the small and young can be overlooked,
But Jesus drew them close, into His hands He took.

They wanted closeness, how trusting children can be,
Now we can do as they did, and climb upon His knee.
For when we trust Jesus like them and go in prayer,
The Father can mold our hearts like His, with care.

Children know their limits, often saying "I can't,"
Surrounded by many giants, and feeling like ants.
The younger they are, the more they ask for help,
We, like them, do well when we see our need and yelp.

We are just like children, we have little we control,
Surrounded by authorities, each dictating our role.
Trusting can be challenging, wondering if we're okay,
But the Father rules them all, and will help us to obey.

Our focus, like a child, can be on what toys we own,
Forgetting the Owner of all is still upon His throne.
He wants us to freely share, offer, and gratefully give,
And when we quarrel with others, learn quickly to forgive.

Our Abba, sweet Daddy, is beside and stands guard,
We can live free and bold, following His charge.
Let's live like a child, and often crawl into His arms,
Taking to Him every concern and any fear that harms.

It's true, His yoke is easy, and His burden is light,
Those who seek truth have less fear in the night.
Jesus said, "The kingdom . . . belongs to such as these,"
Those wanting His presence, to love Him and please.

Jesus said, ". . . for the kingdom
of heaven belongs to such as these."
—Matthew 19:14

How differently would I treat others if I treated them like small children?

How often and for what do I ask God for help?

SIX

How Do You Soothe?

Where do you expend your energy each day? I've realized a lot of my energy has been spent ruminating over situations. I lay them out in my head and consider the possible outcomes, most of which are bad. Perhaps this is an attempt to prepare my heart for disappointment. More times than not, the situations are out of my control and are primarily about choices others are making. I try to ready myself so if one of my drummed-up scenarios comes to pass, I won't be devastated. As warped as it may sound, this ruminating is how I soothe myself in the struggle.

Everyone soothes themselves with something or someone when in emotional pain or distress. We turn to something to stop it or at least lessen it. Sometimes we're aware of how we soothe, but often we are not.

Soothing is something we learn as infants. Infants need comfort when they have emotional or physical needs. If a loving caregiver comes and takes care of their needs when they cry out, they are soothed. As we develop and mature, we all discover ways to soothe ourselves.

Without proper guidance we can learn to soothe ourselves in destructive ways. I've learned my self-soothing has been to attempt to control another person's problems. When this didn't soothe, I'd grab a snack and plop down in front of the TV. When really frustrated, I'd start cleaning the house. At least I could control what I put in my mouth or the cleanliness of my house.

These activities gave me peace, but it was only a false sense of peace. Because, if someone messed with my "peace," I'd respond with frustration that grew into anger and resentment.

All the while, I was unaware of my real problem—me. In attempt to self-soothe my way, I'm assuming the solution can be found within me.

God is called "I Am" for a reason. Because anything and everything we need, He is! He is the only One capable of soothing our brokenness by giving us salvation through His Son. Once saved, He continues to be the only One capable of soothing us in our emotional pain.

When Jesus came in the flesh, He felt pain beyond what we ever will, and every time cried out to His Father to be soothed.

Our struggles are real, as Christ's were. Where do we run? How do we soothe? The Comforter is waiting. He soothes like no other and brings strength, endurance, and real peace to those who cry out to Him.

Do not be anxious about anything, but in everything by prayer and petition, with thanksgiving, present your requests to God. And the peace of God, which transcends all understanding, will guard your hearts and your minds in Christ Jesus.

—Philippians 4:6–7

Soothes and Satisfies

How easy it is in this world to forget or deny,
God is the only One who can completely satisfy.
Looking to another, other than the One above,
To give us what we need, comfort, peace, and love.

Seeking to be soothed in treasures and trinkets we buy,
Assuming this world has something upon which we can rely.
Hoping an object or position will comfort and rectify,
When only God Himself is capable to fulfill and supply.

When misery reaches its fullness, and we're ready to cease,
Acknowledge our helplessness, control's illusion we'll release.
God comforts like no other, only He and His Word can pacify,
Only He empowers to do as He guides, while on Him we rely.

Until we're in heaven, sometimes we'll still forget or deny,
Our neediness as we fall again for the self-sufficiency lie.
Returning to insanity, trying to provide what we need,
Praying without trusting, avoiding His Word to heed.

The more we understand the Father, and how needy we are,
The more we'll embrace our dependency, and hope not to stray far.
As His children we'll make mistakes, like kids we can easily stray,
God is always ready to scoop us up and soothe our hearts without delay.

> For He satisfies the thirsty and
> fills the hungry with good things.
> —Psalm 107:9

To whom or what do I go to for comfort?

Do I struggle with depending on God? If so, why?

SEVEN

Switch It

In Matthew 5–7, Jesus tells His disciples—and us—how to live. His instructions are counter to our impulses and impossible to carry out in our own power. Naturally, we're selfish, self-centered, and lawbreakers (Rom. 2–3). Our bent for wickedness didn't evaporate with salvation. Therefore, we require God's power to obey, to live as He commands.

All we can produce in our own power is something comparable to feces (Isa. 64:6). Our own attempt at living rightly is like a toddler creating art with the paints found in his diaper. What's created may look like a masterpiece of "good works," but it still stinks.

Knowing this, how do we begin? It takes asking God to grow in us a heart like Christ's. In Matthew 7:12, Jesus tells how to interact with others: "So, in everything, do to others what you would have them do to you" (Matt. 7:12).

Jesus, knowing our bent to being self-centered, is teaching us to use it to our advantage—to think about what we'd want and do that. To "do to others what you would have them do to you" takes mentally switching places with others. If we were in their position, how would we want to be treated?

When seeing someone in need, wouldn't we want them to care?

When cut off in traffic, switch places. If we cut someone off, would we want them to lay on the horn, or give us grace and pray for our safety?

What about how we treat a salesperson or checker at the grocery store? Would we want to be ignored?

When a harsh word is said to us, switch and think (or rather remember) how ashamed we felt when we spoke harshly. Wouldn't we want compassion and a willingness to forgive?

This doesn't mean to let everything slide. Jesus also instructs us to reprove and correct others in Christ (Matt. 18:15). We all need to be called out on destructive behavior because it hurts our relationships. But call them out the way we'd want to be treated—gently, compassionately, and privately.

Putting ourselves in another's position helps us see their need for compassion, empathy, and forgiveness. Can you imagine how different our world would be if believers switched their thinking on behavior they encounter all day long? God's plan is for us to live radically different for a purpose.

Living this way can only be done through God's power. When we ask Him, He'll shine brightly through us so others can see Him in us. God's way of living is impossible not to be noticed because it's counter to this world's ways.

Ready to live radically for God? It only takes a switch and a prayer.

> A new command I give you: Love one another. As I have loved you, so you must love one another. By this all men will know that you are my disciples, if you love one another.
>
> —John 13:34–35

Mirror, Mirror

Mirror, mirror on the wall,
Show me first my own fall.
God, I need Your eyes to see
Change You want to make in me.

Impatient with those in a hurry,
Quickly angered by others' fury,
Judging others, judging me,
Trapping others, trapping me.

Gossiping about another's tongue,
Running from a wayward one,
Frustrated by another's attitude,
What I despise, I also do.

Worrying over another's anxiety,
Avoiding those avoiding me,
Resentful if amends refused,
Now another one is due.

By myself I'm helpless to be
Aware of my own depravity.
Only through God's power within
Can You, God, show me my own sin.

Please help me, God, to be
Brokenhearted just like Thee,
By the wrongs I think and do
Transform me to be more like You.

> You, therefore, have no excuse, you who pass judgment on someone else, for at whatever point you judge the other, you are condemning yourself, because you who pass judgment do the same thing.
> —Romans 2:1

> Anyone who listens to the word but does not do what it says is like a man who looks at his face in a mirror and, after looking at himself, goes away and immediately forgets what he looks like.
> —James 1:23–24
>
> Jesus said, "You hypocrite, first take the plank out of your own eye, and then you will see clearly to remove the speck from your brother's eye."
> —Matthew 7:5

How differently would I respond if I switched places with those who sin against me?

When someone's behavior frustrates me, do I see their behavior in my own life?

EIGHT

Jots and Tittles

Do you know what jots and tittles are? A jot is the smallest Hebrew letter. It resembles an apostrophe. A tittle is a tiny mark on a Hebrew letter to keep it from being confused with another letter than looks similar. Jots and tittles are very small but not insignificant. They matter.

Christ talked about jots and tittles when referring to the Old Testament, which is called the Law. Jesus didn't mention the New Testament because it hadn't yet been written. He said, "For assuredly, I say to you, till heaven and earth pass away, one jot or one tittle will by no means pass from the Law till all is fulfilled" (Matt. 5:18 NKJV).

He also said, "And it is easier for heaven and earth to pass away than for one tittle of the Law to fail" (Luke 16:17 NKJV).

Once the New Testament was penned, God made clear the significance of the entire Scriptures by warning, "If anyone adds anything to them, God will add to him the plagues described in this book. And if anyone takes words away from this book of prophecy, God will take away from him his share in the tree of life and in the holy city, which are described in this book" (Rev. 22:18–19).

If every jot and tittle from Genesis to Revelation has been hand placed by God, every word is vital. Our job is to seek and find out why. Reading some parts of Scripture, like the lists of genealogy, can seem boring, but they are vital in proving Jesus came from the family line God promised (Isa. 11:1; Luke 2:1–6)!

God's Word is not only a history book but a book of wisdom on how God wants us to live. That's why "All Scripture is God-breathed and is useful for teaching, rebuking, correcting and training in righteousness" (2 Tim. 3:16).

Those who choose to read the Bible with a teachable heart allow it to do what it's been designed to do—heart work. Within its pages, life is found (John 6:63–69). Those willing to live by it find the abundant life God promises (Ps. 16:11; Matt. 6:33; John 10:10).

Not only is every word purposeful—yes, even in Leviticus!—but also every punctuation. Through it we feel the emotions of those speaking. Mark 9:17–27 tells us of a man bringing his demon-possessed son to Christ in hopes He would heal him. The man told Jesus, "If you can do anything, take pity on us and help us."

Jesus said, "If I can? Everything is possible for him who believes."

The man cried out in anguish, "I do believe; help my unbelief!"

Jesus responded by healing his son before his eyes, revealing a beautiful connection between Jesus and this distraught father.

God is a God of details. His Word is overflowing with them! Are we catching them? God is faithful. He'll show us more and more as we read His Word with a desire to know His heart. Those who do will fall in love with the One who is in love with us and find a stronger faith to cling onto His every word.

The Bible Is Alive

The Bible is perfect and complete,
Through it our holy Creator speaks.
Every word has been perfectly placed,
For every believer, from every race.

Much more than just words on a page,
Holding life and light for every age.
If taken for granted, we forget
It is God's wisdom we reject.

When we lose sight of this truth,
Complacency we allow to take root.
Letting the world and the Enemy's lies
Darken our hearts and blind our eyes.

While our arrogance drives us apart,
Forgetting He died for our stony hearts.
The Book we oft ignore and push aside,
Martyrs gave all for, yet we struggle to abide.

While some Bibles grow dust on a shelf,
Others are treasured more than life itself.
God's Word is still alive and breathing,
Pulsing life into those who are reading.

For the word of God is alive and active.
Sharper than any double-edged sword, it
penetrates even to dividing soul and spirit,
joints and marrow; it judges the thoughts
and attitudes of the heart.
—Hebrews 4:12

How much more do I learn when I read Scripture very slowly?

What would my life be like if I didn't have the Bible?

NINE

What We Do with What We Know

When some people come to faith, they already know much of the Bible, having grown up going to church. This wasn't the case for me. A few years after becoming a believer, I started attending a Bible study called Bible Study Fellowship (BSF). When I joined the class, they were finishing the study of Genesis. With each name I heard being discussed, such as Abraham, Joseph, and others, I thought, who is he? I had a lot to learn.

The more I studied and learned, the more my knowledge mounted; but, unwittingly, so did my arrogance. I thought the more I learned, the more sanctified I was becoming. I knew sanctification is to live more like Christ. But sanctification and a judgmental heart can't coexist. While I had received salvation, deceit was still found in my heart (Jer. 17:9).

I didn't know the sanctification process is a messy one and won't be completed this side of heaven. I didn't yet know "good" behavior done with wrong motives (guilt, coercion, over- dependence on the opinion of others) isn't obedience. When something good is done, the credit should go to God, not me, because the Spirit did the work.

I didn't realize there is still no good to be found in my own nature. I didn't know I wouldn't become a better Christian, not even by learning more of the Bible. So I elevated people who did "good," and judged those who I thought failed to live up to the standard I thought was set by Scripture.

Learning can breed a judgmental attitude toward others. But to be judgmental is evidence we've forgotten what Christ has done for us. When we judge others we deny His blood's work for us, and we deny the reality that remains in our own struggle with our flesh.

The Pharisees were known for being judgmental, and Christ had strong words for them: "Woe to you, teachers of the law and Pharisees, you hypocrites! You are like whitewashed tombs, which look beautiful on the outside but on the inside are full of dead men's bones and everything unclean. In the same way, on the outside you appear to people as righteous but on the inside you are full of hypocrisy and wickedness" (Matt. 23:27–28).

Being judgmental chooses hate not love, smugness not empathy, criticism not humility. It requires forgetting or denying our own sinful bent. We may have different sins than another, but all sins require Christ's blood. We harm others and our witness when criticizing them with words, actions, or by facial expressions. That's why Jesus spoke so harshly about it (Matt. 7:1–5).

We act upon what we know is important, but actions alone don't prove faith in Jesus. Believers and unbelievers alike attend church, study the Bible, and serve others. What we do with what we know and why we do it are what matters. God cares about the heart.

It can be painful to discover how much we do to feel good about ourselves and/or to be seen favorably by others. But self-examination is necessary in the sanctification process—that is, when it leads to confession and dependency on God to do what only He can do—and makes lasting changes in us for His glory (Matt. 5:16).

The more we know about God, and our tendency to do the wrong thing, the more grateful for Him we'll become. The more we'll realize there's so much we don't know and grateful we belong to Him who knows all. Gratitude grows a desire to surrender to His way of thinking so He can build an attitude of compassion and empathy in us, toward others as well as ourselves.

Knowing and Doing

Knowing and doing are not the same thing,
It takes doing what's known for faith to be seen.
We can know Scripture, God's Word, real and true,
Yet not allow the Spirit to transform us to live anew.
If God's Word is known but stays only in our heads,
We may act morally good but we mirror the dead.
It takes a dependency to obey with a pure heart,
This kind of living reveals we've been set apart.

Therefore, faith without action is no faith at all,
We'll stumble but with repentance we're safe to fall.
God doesn't expect perfection when living for Him,
We won't look for it either when confessing our sin.
Only the Spirit can empower to live just and true,
And fill us with God's peace, joy, and patience too.
God provides all that's needed for the willing who seek,
To do what's made known, accepting they're weak.

The Enemy's goal is to keep the knowing undone,
For Satan knows the doing is what displays the Son.
When the doing is hard and God's power is sought,
Courage is given to live out what's been taught.
All glory is God's in whatever good thing we do,
May many be encouraged to choose obedience too.
The world is watching and through us God can shine,
Empowered to do what's known as with Him we align.

This is the word of the LORD to Zerubbabel: "Not by might nor by power, but by my Spirit," says the LORD Almighty.
—Zechariah 4:6

Do not merely listen to the word, and so deceive yourselves. Do what it says.
—James 1:22

Compared to when I first trusted in Christ as my Savior, how have I changed?

Do I find it easier to give grace or criticism of myself or others?

TEN

Learning to Lean

My friend Jerry and I were discussing what God had been doing in our lives. With his permission, I'm sharing what he told me.

Jerry said he'd been struggling with 1 Peter 5:6–7. The Message paraphrase says: "So be content with who you are, and don't put on airs. God's strong hand is on you; he'll promote you at the right time. Live carefree before God; he is most careful with you."

His struggle was with "God's strong hand is on you" because he visualized His hand bearing down on his shoulder like that of a stern parent. As Jerry prayed about this, God brought to mind a daily routine he had with his young son. When Jerry's son brushed his teeth, Jerry would stand behind him. His son would lean back on him, and Jerry would place his strong hand on his son's chest. What a beautiful picture of trust and dependency!

May we, as God's children, lean often on our Father, the One we fell upon to give us eternal life. Knowing what He's done for us, it would be easy to think that leaning on God will come naturally for us, but it doesn't. Scripture says we have no hope of carrying these things out without Him, so really there is no reason to think we should. Both our flesh and the ways of this sinful world entice us to lean on ourselves and others, not God. But whatever or whomever we lean on (other than God) is fleeting and unable to carry our needy heart's load.

Only God is always there. He, like no one else, is constant, always present, and always available for us to lean on. He doesn't grow weary, and He's not fickle like we can be. We're in desperate need of His strength to do as we should, even when we want to! Yet we either forget or deny this throughout our days. We may feel emotionally strong and invincible but are just one circumstance away from a meltdown. When we feel spiritually strong, we're really blinded by pride. Even when we feel physical strong, we're not immune to injury.

But God's strong hand never weakens, His broken heart never implodes, and He never loses His temper. When we see His anger in Scripture, it's not a meltdown but what's needed to melt the hearts of those resisting His goodness. God strength is eternal and has been proven by each fulfilled promise. His strength never falters and His desire for our dependency on Him never fades. It's the best place for us to dwell. Leaning on Him opens our hearts to His transforming work. So lean in, ask for His understanding, rest in His timing, and He will make your way straight.

> Trust in the LORD with all your heart, and lean not on your own understanding; in all your ways acknowledge him, and he will make your paths straight. Do not be wise in your own eyes; fear the LORD and shun evil. This will bring health to your body and nourishment to your bones.
> —Proverbs 3:5–8

Leaning on the Lord

When leaning upon the Lord, He empowers us to live differently,
But until His own reach heaven, we won't do it continually.
Our flesh and this world will tempt us to lean instead into them,
Both God's heart and ours are broken when we don't lean on Him.
When we lean on the ways of the world, we hold the burden's weight,
Christ tells us to cast it upon Him; our heart rests when prostrate.

With God's strong hand upon us we're secure and forever His child,
When we lean into His presence we reflect His heart good and mild.
Leaning is letting the Lord work, to do what only His power can do,
Leaning is surrendering to His ways, trusting Him to be faithful and true.
His fruit is produced when we lean, possible only through His power,
Living life with this kind of dependency, makes demons shudder and cower.

Leaning on the Lord occurred at salvation, resting in His promises true,
When first leaning upon Jesus, we saw ourselves from God's point of view.
Leaning not upon our own understanding, resting instead in who is real,
Jesus, God's only Son, faith in His death for us gives power to kneel.
With salvation, leaning brought peace, but how quickly we forget to rely,
The best way to live as believers, is to lean on Christ until we die.

Rejoice in the Lord always, I will say it again: Rejoice! Let your gentleness be evident to all. The Lord is near. Do not be anxious about anything, but in everything by prayer and petition, with thanksgiving present your requests to God. And the peace of God, which transcends all understanding, will guard your hearts and your minds in Christ Jesus.
—Philippians 4:4–7

Humble yourselves, therefore, under God's mighty hand, that he may lift you up in due time. Cast all your anxieties on him because he cares for you.
—1 Peter 5:6–7

Do I trust myself and others more or God? Why?

When did I last lean on God? What were the results?

ELEVEN

The Pain of Regret

Isn't regret painful? Most of us have experienced regret—that realization of something you'd wished you'd done or not done. We've all been given opportunity to do something not knowing it was the only opportunity we'd have.

Years ago, a friend and I were making plans to get together so our kids could play. At the end of the conversation, another mother walked up to us. I felt an internal nudge to invite her to what we'd just planned. But I ignored the nudge because I wanted my friend all to myself. After a little chitchat, we parted and each carried on with our day. The mother who had walked up to us was pregnant and nearly full term. A few days later I received a call saying she had delivered a healthy child, but had died during childbirth!

My immediate response was, "No!" This event was over twenty-five years ago, but the memory is strong. My regret was I couldn't go back and do what I hadn't done.

Later that year I was asked to become a leader in a Bible study I was attending. The position intimidated me and I felt ill-equipped, because I was. I didn't realize the leaders in this study are trained every week in how to lead. I also didn't realize they didn't have the rigid expectations of me that I had.

I made up an excuse (a gentle word for a lie) and declined the invitation. My brief feeling of relief was replaced with regret; it ate at me for weeks. Thankfully, the leader asked me again saying, "This time pray over your answer." There was no need. The Spirit had been clearly convicting me.

Regret has the potential to be a great teacher, if we let it. The more painful the regret, the less likely we'll repeat the action that brought regret. God has used the pain of my selfishness to motivate me to welcome others warmly. Sadly, I've lost the opportunity to confess and have a redo with the mother who passed. But I thank God she was a sister in Christ; when I see her again, I can ask her forgiveness.

There is one event coming when there will be no opportunities to redo it is when our Lord and Savior returns. How we respond now will lead to joy or regret. "And now, dear children, continue in him, so that when he appears we may be confident and unashamed before him at his coming" (1 John 2:28).

How we live today is all we have. As believers we have chosen to lay aside our own desires to live our lives for God, but we will never do this perfectly. It's hard not to wake up with big plans for our day. Yet, I have found that regrets often come if I hold on to those plans too tightly. What we want and what we think we need beg correction because only God knows what is best.

Do you need a redo? God's mercy is never ending. "Because of the LORD's great love we are not consumed, for his compassions never fail. They are new every morning; great is your faithfulness" (Lam. 3:22–23). All we need to do is repent to experience His forgiveness and leave our regrets in the past behind us. Then ask God to give us a willingness to do His will and show us someone today whom we can serve.

When We Fail

When we fail greatly it is used to help us see,
On our own we're helpless, needing Christ-dependency.
Failure helps believers see we can't do life on our own,
Remember our beginning, we once had a heart of stone.

After failing greatly, a stronger bond is made,
Drawing us even closer to our God who saved.
Failure helps us cling to God's mercy and grace,
Reminding more often our constant lowly place.

Having failed greatly, a heart of gratitude is grown,
God knew our sins coming, still chose us as His own.
Never will we understand the generous mind of God,
Each failure increases the amount of time we're awed.

Great failure happened also to believers in the past,
Given to us as examples to complete what He has asked.
Peter shows us in the garden and in fear denying Christ,
Failures made Peter want obedience the rest of his life.

Pain of past mistakes helps us to live a life of reverence,
Hoping not to repeat wrongs, grateful for His benevolence.
Regret is a great teacher and stays with us for life,
Helping to spur us on in devotion and sacrifice.

If our failure is not evaluated, to learn what was taught,
Ignoring it isn't helpful, guilty feelings can't be forgot.
All is covered for the believer, His grace and mercy given,
For the wayward believer who's failed, has fully been forgiven.

"Come now, let us settle the matter," says the
LORD. "Though your sins are like scarlet, they
shall be as white as snow; though they are red as
crimson, they shall be like wool."
—Isaiah 1:18

How do I feel about the Lord's return to earth?

Do I have a fear of failing? If so or not, why?

TWELVE

Life Sentence

Have you heard of Angola Prison? It's the largest maximum-security prison in America. It holds over five thousand murderers, rapists, armed robbers, and habitual felons. Most inmates have been given a life sentence with no possibility of parole. Before 1995 it was known as the bloodiest prison in America because of regularly occurring violence. But God transformed this prison one soul at a time, beginning with the new warden, Burl Cain.

Burl, a believer in Christ, was a no-nonsense man. A few months after he began working at Angola, he witnessed an execution. Burl saw executions as just part of the job of carrying out justice. As the man died, Burl was struck with regret for failing to talk to him about Jesus. Burl vowed that day that it wouldn't happen again. He also placed a Bible in every cell and offered Bible studies to anyone interested in attending. In addition, Burl spoke with a local seminary about offering remote training to inmates desiring a divinity degree.

God, through His Word and His Spirit, began to transform the atmosphere of this prison. It went from being the bloodiest prison in America to a prison where violence is rare. Blood on the walls has been replaced with Scripture. Most inmates now are described as courteous and respectful. Six churches meet within its walls and are pastored by trained inmates. Others who have been trained are sent out in teams of two as missionaries to other prisons to plant churches. All of the biblical training and materials have been provided by private donations and do not use tax dollars. Prisoners now have hope and the desire to make something of themselves even if they never again see the outside.

Do you feel imprisoned, as if your situation is a life sentence? Whatever our circumstances, even if our situation does not change, just as these fellow brothers in Christ, we can let God change us. When we open up God's Word with a teachable heart, God will do His transforming work. God asks of us to do the same as the prisoners: read, pray, and be patient. Over time, like them, we'll see God empower us to live differently. Within the walls of your home, when God's Word is applied through God's power, He'll bring hope and joy where there was none found.

For the word of God is living and active. Sharper than any double-edged sword, it penetrates even to dividing soul and spirit, joints and marrow; it judges the thoughts and attitudes of the heart. Nothing in all creation is hidden from God's sight. Everything is uncovered and laid bare before the eyes of Him to whom we must give account.
—Hebrews 4:12–13

All Scripture is God-breathed and is useful for teaching, rebuking, correcting and training in righteousness, so that the man of God may be thoroughly equipped for every good work.
—2 Timothy 3:16–17

Sunday Is Coming

When life looks like Good Friday, hold on to what you know,
Don't allow what looks hopeless to toss you to and fro.
Resurrection Sunday's coming, don't wait in defeat,
The Son is still shining, don't listen to dark deceit.

On your knees talk to the Father, as Jesus did in distress,
Pour out all fear and anxiety, what God knows confess.
Ask the Father for courage to seek His will as Jesus did,
Arise and face the day with God, choosing in Him to be hid.

Trust this moment has purpose, nothing will go to waste,
Let Him strip away the whys, so His glory you foretaste.
Fix your eyes on the Father, the character you know of Him,
Fill your mind with truth, and chase away lies with a hymn.

Circumstances don't dictate joy, it's the other way around,
When crushed by opposition, do as Paul and Silas were found.
Unjustly put in prison, after being flogged and bound by chains,
In dark of night sang hymns, not a reflection of their domain.

Friday isn't forever, though it seems Sunday will never come,
There's a battle you can't see, the enemy hopes you'll succumb.
Wait and watch for God is near, this isn't the end of your story,
Trust He's working though you can't see, all for His glory.

He fell to the ground and prayed that if possible the hour might pass from him. . . . "Yet not what I will, but what you will . . . the Scriptures must be fulfilled."
—Mark 14:35, 49

About midnight Paul and Silas were praying and singing hymns to God, and the other prisoners were listening to them.
—Acts 16:25

How am I responding to my situation?

What do I do while I'm waiting to see what God will do in my situation?

THIRTEEN

May "I'm Done" Become "Well Done"

"I'm done." Have you said these words? I have when worn slick by a trial that seemed to have no end.

I've said them to a sister in Christ.

I've said them to a counselor.

But who I needed to say them to is God.

In those times I needed more than perseverance; I needed God's perspective.

How does my perspective shift to His? By praising Him. Yes, you read it correctly, by praise. His attributes spoken aloud and meditated on draw the eyes of a weary heart from hopeless to the One who "in him all things hold together" (Col. 1:17). He's holding me, and if you trust Jesus took your punishment, He is holding you too.

How do I know praising God shifts a perspective? I've experienced it. But you don't have to take my word. It's scattered all through Scripture.

In psalm after psalm we read how David is at his wit's end, and then he belts out praise. As he questions and complains, he begins to remind his soul of God's character.

My favorite example of this shift is from Habakkuk. Habakkuk struggles with the serious injustice being done all around him.

Habakkuk was done. The Lord's response to Habakkuk's prayer is hard to hear. God tells him the injustice isn't over and it's going to get even worse. Habakkuk then reminds his own soul of some of God's attributes. Habakkuk ends his struggle with what I need to remember. He prays, "I will stand at my watch and station myself on the ramparts; I will look to see what he will say to me" (Hab. 2:1).

Rampart is not a word we often use today. It's a broad elevation or mound of earth raised as a fortification to serve as a defense. In doing this, Habakkuk is seeking the shift and God brings it. God tells Habakkuk to "Write down the revelation and make it plain on tablets so that a herald may run with it" (Hab. 2:2), to share the hope that was coming.

God will make all things right. He may have told Habakkuk more injustice is coming, but He also says justice is coming and woe to those in rebellion when it comes.

Nothing in Habakkuk's situation had changed and worse was promised. His environment didn't change but Habakkuk had. What brought this change? God's unchanging character was spoken. As Habakkuk spoke what he knew of God, he was encouraged to wait.

He didn't wait in the pit. He planted himself on the rampart of his soul—His defender and source of strength. From this position, remembering on whom He was standing, he could better see God's perspective.

I won't see all of God's perfect perspective in this life, but as I learn to do as Habakkuk did, He shows me what I need to see.

God does His biggest work in trials. Through trials we're forced to realize the truth—we're powerless to change the brokenness of this world.

When feeling done we have a choice. We can keep looking at our own perspective or seek God's. Our perspective is usually skewed and slanted in our favor, which works against us. His perspective is perfect. No matter how much we mess up, He won't give up on us.

Our job is to ask Him to change us and get out of His way. That means asking for change without an agenda. God alone can bring positive change in our lives. We choose how miserable we'll be while waiting for it.

Are you desperate for change? Meditate on who God is and it will come. We'll learn like Habakkuk to trust that He's working and has a perfect plan. We need only set our hearts on His. Then when we're really done in this life, may we hear, "Well done" (Matt. 25:21).

Thy Will Be Done

There is no peace like when someone
Can pray and mean "Thy will be done."
Just as in the garden did God's Son,
Who gave over His will till the battle was won.
Face set like flint, on the cross He'd stay,
Even when his Father had to look away.
He knew God's will included the sin,
All of our wrongs, heaped upon Him.
Putting our punishment fully upon,
His One and Only Son for us to be won.

Our victory of being bought for God,
Our only hope, loved though flawed.
This kind of love for depraved man,
Inconceivable, but was God's plan.
Knowing this helps me also to pray,
"Thy will be done" in my pain today.
I don't need to understand the "why"
Of why did God send Jesus to die?
Why did He choose to love the lost,
Giving life through Christ's cross?

What I can seek is to trust His view,
Just like Jesus on the cross had to do.
Dying to self throughout the day,
Seeking His will, trusting His way.
Depending upon the truth that He,
Will fulfill perfectly His plan for me.
I don't have to grasp what God is doing,
Peace comes as I follow the Spirit's wooing.
Strengthen me God, to accept and not run,
Trusting as Jesus did, "Thy will be done."

He went away again the second time, and prayed, "My Father, if it is not possible for this cup to be taken away unless I drink it, may your will be done."
—Matthew 26:42

Being confident of this, that he who began a good work in you will carry it on to completion until the day of Christ Jesus.
—Philippians 1:6

When has praise changed my perspective?

What does God want me to put to the side for Him?

FOURTEEN

Answering the Questioner

When asked a hard question about God, I've found it easy to panic, feeling ill-equipped to answer. If the question comes with heated emotions, I've felt even more responsible to answer in a way that changes the questioner's perspective of God. If the inerrancy of Scripture has been doubted, I've felt a need to defend it and prove its accuracy. If God's goodness has been doubted, I've felt it my job to defend His character.

God has taught me that I'm the one who is unknowingly questioning who He is and forgetting my own nature as well as the nature of the questioner.

God Himself needs no defending or proof of His existence. He's already made it clear (Rom. 1:20). It's both futile and arrogant to assume any "right words" can change another's way of thinking (1 Cor. 2:14).

What we've been called to defend isn't God but our faith. "Always be prepared to give an answer to everyone who asks you to give the reason for the hope that you have. But do this with gentleness and respect" (1 Peter 3:15).

We can't make doubters trust God's Word. Hearts are hard and minds are closed until God opens them (Eph. 2:1–6). We aren't asked to open closed minds, but only to be ready to answer when they ask, and ready to preach the truth about God at all times (2 Tim. 4:2). We're responsible for being in God's Word (1 Thess. 2:13; 2 Tim. 3:16–17).

The Spirit guides believers who are willing to be used. He'll not only guide what to say but when to say it (Matt. 10:19–20).

No question threatens God. Remembering who God is and our need for Him softens our hearts, making us approachable to the questioner. An eternal soul stands before us. We're answering not a question, but a questioner. This is hard to keep in mind when questions come with venom. Whatever the motive of the questioner, pain or anger, or the desire to win an argument, God can use it to drawn them to Himself. When we keep God in the forefront of our minds, He'll enable us to respond with love, compassion, and respect.

Those who love God and others open themselves up to be used greatly by Him and for Him. He'll bring opportunities to answer hard questions from hard questioners. He'll even use the willing who happen to be in a terrible mood when the opportunity arises.

That's what happened to me when I was asked to visit someone in the hospital. The person requesting didn't know I'd been praying for this man's salvation for years. We'd had spiritual conversations in the past but each had ended with his refusal of God's Word.

I agreed to go but was in a foul mood when I went. When I arrived in his hospital room, the first words out of his mouth were, "Vicky, how do you know you're going to heaven?"

In an instance God melted my heart and filled me with step-by-step words. We spoke for a while, and he responded to the way of salvation with venom (John 14:6). Yet the whole time I felt a depth of love and compassion for him that could only come from God. Then, abruptly, he stopped our conversation. I told him I loved him and felt the Spirit's guidance to leave.

When I left his room I began shaking, but I was filled with peace. God had thrown His seed of truth, and He alone knew if it would turn into faith. This man's hard heart saddened me, but what the Spirit had done in me was indescribable. I wonder if this is how the apostles felt when they spoke to crowds as vessels being used by God.

God does it all! He provides His Word, His Spirit's power, opportunities, and step-by-step guidance. He even provides a change of attitude when needed. Remembering this removes the panic when hard questions come. God provides His peace as we are merely being vessels for Him to address the questioner.

Transformed to Witness

Nothing shines the glory of God like a transformed life,
No longer as they were, choosing self to sacrifice.
More caught up with who God is, wanting all to see,
Christ's work upon the cross was to set sinners free.
Grateful for what He's done, and seeking what's in store,
As well as Spirit empowered, to live differently than before.
When others start to notice, and wonder what's been done,
An opportunity is opened for them to hear of the Son.

Fear to share will dissipate when our gaze goes to above,
For self can't be the focus when the heart is full of love.
Awe replaces fear, excitement takes anxiety's place,
Wondering who else will get to rest in God's embrace.
A heart soft toward sinners where judgment had been,
More tender toward the Spirit to see and confess sin.
With Christ there are no barriers, none out of reach,
Be available to love in action and sometimes by speech.

A growing countenance of peace, trusting in His plan,
Remembering evil is no threat for the great I Am.
Words are often used by God to bring sinners to Christ,
But mostly it's behavior and joy in believers' sacrifice.
In a heart sold out for what God loves, He can be seen,
With no thought of self so only Christ is in between.
The unsaved may not be ready to accept Christ that day,
But another transformed life may be soon sent their way.

And we, who with unveiled faces all reflect the Lord's glory, are being transformed into his likeness with ever-increasing glory, which comes from the Lord, who is the Spirit.
—2 Corinthians 3:18

Therefore, we do not lose heart. Though outwardly we are wasting away, yet inwardly we are being renewed day by day.
—2 Corinthians 4:16

How do I feel and respond when asked questions about God?

What or whom am I focusing on when I'm asked a question?

FIFTEEN

Take Him at His Word

*H*ave you ever been terrified one minute, then in an instant sure the threat was gone?

Years ago, I was about to drive our daughters to school when I remembered I forgot something inside. As I was walking back into the house, I heard a vehicle pull up behind our van. One of the two men in the truck stepped out and began walking briskly toward our garage. I stood frozen in the doorway of our home.

He saw me and continued to walk toward me, like a man on a mission. You may be thinking I watch too many detective shows, but it's amazing how quickly thoughts can race through your mind when you're terrified.

I can't shut the door to trigger the alarm because I'll lose sight of my children. Do they know my girls are in the van? If they're quiet will they be safe? Are we going to be harmed or killed?

Suddenly he froze and said, "I have the wrong house." He quickly turned around, walked just as briskly to the truck, got in and they drove away.

I was rattled and shaking, but immediately knew we were safe. How could I go from terror to feeling confident that we were protected? Only by the hand of God. Only God could flood me with a peace and freedom from fear that didn't leave once the adrenalin was gone. My assurance continued throughout the day as I dropped off my girls at school and continued the day as if nothing had happened.

This experience reminds me of what happened in Cana, as recorded in John 4:46–54. An official from Capernaum had a son who was gravely ill to the point of death. Hearing Jesus was in Cana, he traveled the sixteen miles to ask Jesus to heal his son. When the official found Jesus, he begged Him, "Sir, come down before my child dies."

Jesus responded, "You may go. Your son will live."

You'd think the official would have run back home to verify his son was well, but he didn't. How do we know this? The walk back would have taken a few hours. If he'd been on horseback, he'd have returned even quicker. Instead, he returned home the next day. On his way, his servants met him with the news of his son's healing. When the official asked what time his son got better, they said, "'The fever left him yesterday at the seventh hour.' Then the father realized that this was the exact time at which Jesus had said to him, 'Your son will live'" (John 4:52–53).

What had the father been doing before he went home? Taking care of business? It wasn't as if he didn't care about his son. He proved his devotion to his son the day before. Being a man of high authority, he'd publicly begged help from a common man from Nazareth called Jesus. Scripture proves this man's faith as it records, he took Jesus at His word. He didn't need to see his son for confirmation of his healing, but God gave it to him anyway with news of his son's time of healing. This confirmation solidified his faith and brought his household to faith in Christ as well.

May we too remember who God is and take Him at His Word. May we preach His Word to our souls especially when things look terrifying. Things may not work out as we want, but one thing is certain. God is faithful so we too can take Him at His Word.

We are hard pressed on every side, but not crushed; perplexed, but not in despair; persecuted, but not abandoned; struck down, but not destroyed.
—2 Corinthians 4:8–9

For our light and momentary troubles are achieving for us an eternal glory that far outweighs them all. So we fix our eyes not on what is seen, but on what is unseen. For what is seen is temporary, but what is unseen is eternal.
—2 Corinthians 4:17–18

Anchor for My Soul

Not shifting sand but solid Rock, the Anchor for my soul,
Christ fulfills God's every promise, and He makes me whole.
When my mind is stayed upon, God's Word I do not move,
Will not waver from the One, my hardships only prove.
He is everything He claims to be, His promises are real,
No matter what happens in life, or how I unstable I feel.

Doubt, fear, anxiety, strong desire to be in control,
When forgetting my Stabilizer, the Lover of my soul.
Preach the Gospel to myself, refresh and reset my mind,
My troubles are no threat to Him, He'll empower me to align.
He'll guide and redirect me, teaching much from when I fall,
No hurt or failure is wasted, He'll even use them in His call.

Daily fill my mind with Truth, so His Word can seep,
Into every crevice exposing lies, believed and rooted deep.
As more of His promises are read, and each one is received,
These can be the Sword drawn, when the enemy deceives.
Can't trust my own perspective, God's alone will I seek,
My own nature is destruction, embrace that I'm weak.

His grace is sufficient, He gives the weary rest,
He is always available, and found when my quest.
His mercies never ceasing, He rescues me from me,
His hand of discipline is love, growing my dependency.
Faithful even when I'm not, leading me to see sin to confess,
With repentance He empowers, to crave His righteousness.

I reflect whom I love more, when I choose self and sin,
His love never diminishes, His patience never wears thin.
He knew what He was getting when He went to Calvary,
He loves me where I am, but too much to leave me be.
My Rock, the Anchor for my soul never ever tries to leave,
I may forget to Whom I belong but He never forgets me.

We have this hope as anchor for the soul, firm and secure. It enters the inner sanctuary behind the curtain, where our Forerunner, Jesus, has entered on our behalf.
—Hebrews 6:17–20

What truth about God do I need to take in completely even if life looks contrary?

What truth anchor's me when waves of trials crash?

Sixteen

The Good Shepherd

In John 10, Jesus refers to Himself as our shepherd. We are His own, His sheep. This may seem strange to us who are not around flocks and shepherds, but the visual teaching wasn't lost to those listening to Jesus. Where they lived, sheep and shepherds were commonly seen. When we understand the relationship between shepherds and sheep during the Bible times, we can see the wisdom and tenderness of these verses and other such as in Isaiah 40:10–11, Psalm 23, and Mark 6:34.

A good shepherd would sacrifice physical comfort, sleep, and time with their family in order to take care of his sheep. If, when a lamb was born, its mother was unable to care for it or rejected it, the shepherd would bottle feed it and keep it close. When the lamb was strong enough, it would be placed with the rest of the flock. When the shepherd called, lambs that had been bottle fed were first to come because they'd learned to trust the shepherd.

Have you been neglected or rejected by someone who couldn't or wouldn't care for you? Let God's care for you build trust in Him, and answer when He calls.

Two of the tools that a good shepherd would carry were a staff (stick up to six feet long) and a rod (sturdy club). The staff was used as a walking stick and to guide the sheep. The rod was used for protection. Sheep have no defenses, making them very vulnerable, so the rod was used to fight off wild animals.

Sometimes though, the rod was used to break the leg of a sheep that kept wandering away from the flock. Wandering made them easy prey. Breaking a leg sounds cruel, but the alternative was death. Once the rod had been applied, the sheep was then carried upon the shepherd's shoulders until its leg mended. The time spent close to the shepherd built a connection, helping it stay close once healed. Jesus is the Good Shepherd and only disciplines out of love. When the rod is used, it breaks His heart too, but is done to protect us from our own destruction (Prov. 3:11–12).

The rod was also used as a gate. At the end of the day, the shepherd would gather the sheep in a pen. The rod was held at the doorway of the pen. Before each sheep came into the pen, it was stopped and inspected for any wounds that needed to be addressed before being allowed to go into the pen.

We also need to be inspected (Ps. 139:23–24). We can ask the Father to expose emotional wounds caused by others' sins against us as well as wounds we cause to others. In doing this, God can heal us from the inside out.

We are as needy and defenseless as sheep. Thankfully, we have a Good Shepherd who gave His life for us! He knows us better than we know ourselves. He's trustworthy and promises to draw close to those willing to draw near to Him. Those who do draw near find an inexpressible intimacy with Him because they've spent time on His shoulders, healing.

> He heals the brokenhearted and binds up their wounds.
> —Psalm 147:3

Your Rod and Your Staff

Your rod and staff they comfort me, through both You refine,
The staff less painful than the rod, but both help me align.
When willing I feel Your guidance, gently nudging where to go,
But when my stubborn heart's unyielding, my will requires a blow.
Your staff You'd rather use, but filled with pride I'm numb,
I dismiss the Spirit's nudges, Your gentle voice saying, "Come."

The rod used against the enemy must then be used on me,
It hurts us both to break my will when I'm blind to my depravity.
When I think I can shepherd myself, destruction is all I bring,
Proving the need for You to break my will, teaching me to cling.
Upon Your shoulders I'm carefully placed, and carried as I mend,
As You reacquaint me with Yourself, my God, my Lord, and Friend.

Looking back at my life, I can see for my good You used the rod,
When I determined my way was right, forgetting my way is flawed.
My wanderings have brought much pain, to me, and others in my life,
Through the rod You've helped me understand the reason for the strife.
Your rod I don't desire, but when required for change to take place,
I've learned You're as gentle as possible, and comfort me with grace.

The LORD is my shepherd, I shall not be in want. He makes me lie down in green pastures, he leads me beside quiet waters, he restores my soul. He guides me in paths of righteousness for his name's sake. Even though I walk through the valley of the shadow of death, I will fear no evil, for you are with me; your rod and your staff, they comfort me. You prepare a table before me in the presence of my enemies. You anoint my head with oil; my cup overflows. Surely goodness and love will follow me all the days of my life, and I will dwell in the house of the LORD forever.

—Psalm 23:1–6

What have I gained or lost by ignoring the Spirit's nudges?

What have I gained by resting on my Shepherd's shoulders?

SEVENTEEN

God Is Still in Control

Are you walking with the Lord, seeking His will, and still feel like your life is out of control? It can appear that way sometimes. But throughout Scripture we see God's hand on His people. Things may have looked out of control, but God had it all in control. It's the same for us today.

When Jesus began His ministry, many did not want what He had to offer. They tried to silence and destroy Him. The crowds even picked up stones, tried to push Him off a cliff, and tried to grab Him to arrest Him. Each time they failed, until it was His time. Jesus wasn't "taken under their control" until control was given.

In the garden, Jesus made it clear who was really in control. Read John 18:1–11 to get a clear picture of the sovereignty of God. Judas, thinking he was in control, led a detachment of soldiers (up to six hundred men thinking they were in control). Some officials from the chief priests and Pharisees (each thinking he was in control) came to arrest Jesus—who had complete control.

Jesus asked them, "Who is it you want?"

They said, "Jesus of Nazareth."

Look what happened when Jesus responded, "I am He." All of them coming to arrest Jesus (including Judas) drew back and fell to the ground. Drawing back kept them from falling upon the Lord Himself!

It was clear Jesus was in command. As they all gathered themselves and stood back up to face Jesus, again He asked them, "Who is it you want?"

Were they rattled? Was Jesus reminding them of their orders to arrest Him? As they arrested Him, Jesus continued to take charge, telling them, "Let these men go," referring to His disciples.

Full of fear, Peter in his great love for Jesus, apparently forgot who Jesus was and what had just happened. He attempted to protect his Lord by drawing his sword. Peter's swing did damage, but Jesus took command of that too by touching the man's ear and healing him.

Does your life seem out of control? Does it seem things are going wrong and there is no hope? Read John 18 and see that what seems out of control and hopeless isn't, because the orchestrator of time and space has it all. Keep looking to Him. Keep asking Him to give you eyes to see what is really happening.

God has a perfect plan for our lives, and it is a great one. He wastes nothing, even when we've made decisions that we think have wrecked our lives. God alone does what seem impossible. With Him all things are possible (Matt. 19:26). He'll hold us together even during the most difficult circumstances, using all to mold and shape us, refine and grow us. The deeper our trust in His sovereignty grows, the quicker we'll give over our illusion of control to the One who already has it.

> I know that you can do all things; no plan of yours can be thwarted.
> —Job 42:2
>
> He is before all things, and in him all things hold together.
> —Colossians 1:17

Who Is in Control

Whenever we are fearful, there's a sure solution to …
Drown our fear and anxiety, let truth come into view.
We need to bravely answer two questions honestly,
These questions help remind us of our own dependency.

"Who is in control?" Here's a hint, the answer's God,
Well then, "Do I trust Him or someone who is flawed?"
The first question is easy for the humbled and saved,
The second one is harder because we're still depraved.

Attempting to navigate all the things that come at us,
When we doubt God, in ourselves we've placed our trust.
We trust our Savior completely to take our sins away,
If He can do the greater, He can surely guide our way.

Living in this world, it's hard to continue there,
When more trouble comes at us, we are unaware.
How quickly fear can return and settle in our soul,
Time to ask the question again, "Who is in control?"

Another question is helpful, if we'd only add,
"What are some of His traits?" all being ironclad.
Pondering upon them brings God back into view,
Correcting our thinking that fear of man can skew.

> When anxiety was great within me, your consolation brought joy to my soul.
> —Psalm 94:19
>
> So do not fear, for I am with you; do not be dismayed, for I am your God. I will strengthen you and help you; I will uphold you with my righteous right hand.
> —Isaiah 41:10

What in my life seems out of control?

How does nature continue to prove God is in control?

EIGHTEEN

Let's Take a Walk

Hebrews 11 is known as the "Hall of Faith," a collection of men and women living out what they believe. Their faith wasn't defined by one event, even though about some that's all we know. Their faith was how they were known then and throughout history. Let's take a walk down this hall and look at a few.

By faith Noah built an ark as God directed (Gen. 6–7). He'd never heard of rain, a flood, or an ark. These words were foreign to him, and he didn't have Google. But he believed God, and that was enough for him to obey. He believed God's warning. Destruction was coming, and the ark was his and his family's salvation. Noah worked hard for possibly one hundred years (Gen. 5:32; 7:6). Talk about perseverance! Noah was given instructions, but he had to choose over and over again to continue to trust and obey. He's called a "preacher of righteousness" (2 Pet. 2:5), yet no one except his family believed and entered the ark.

Obedience can come with discouragement. When I am weary or discouraged, I need to take heart and remember my faith in God is the same as Noah's! When God asks something of me that seems confusing, I need to remember He knows fully and that's enough. If it seems impossible, is it really impossible for Him?

By faith Abraham believed God's promise that his barren wife would give him a son. He had to wait twenty-five years to receive

Isaac (Gen. 21). He didn't wait completely patiently, but following his wife's bad advice, lay with Hagar and paid for it dearly (Gen. 16). But Abraham still trusted God would provide. He lay with his barren wife who was ninety years old and received his son Isaac. God rewards the heart of obedience knowing obedience won't be free of fallbacks. Abraham learned from his failures to trust God even more. Abraham showed the depth of his faith when he was willing to sacrifice his most precious Isaac (Gen. 22). He didn't know what God would do but trusted Him.

How are trials revealing my faith? Do I need more faith? What's keeping me from asking? (See James 1:5.)

By faith Rahab welcomed in strangers and risked her life by hiding them (Josh. 2). Why? Because she believed the stories she'd heard. News had spread that the God of the Israelites had parted the Red Sea so they could escape their enemy. Once safe on the other side, God released the waters to fall on their enemy. Rahab believed what she heard and knew the land where she lived had been promised to God's people. Knowing her neighbors wouldn't give it up willingly, fear could have immobilized her. Instead, she proved her faith by welcoming the spies into her home as she had God into her heart. She had laid down her old beliefs and now told the spies to lie down so she could hide them under flax. She risked her life, and God not only spared her and her household, but also grafted her into the genealogy of Jesus.

God always outgives what's given. What wrong beliefs am I willing to lay down?

This hall of faith continues to be added to today. The same Author and Perfecter of their faith is the Lord of those who are sure of what's hoped for and certain of what's not seen (Heb. 11:1). This is faith. God provides it, and will deepen it if we let Him.

Ask and He'll give the faith of Noah to believe even when it doesn't make sense. He'll give the faith of Abraham to believe His promises. He'll give courage to lay down a belief and join those who share with others what God has done. Those listening may be like Rahab who believed what's heard. If they want to hear more, take them for a walk down the Hall of Faith.

Freedom to Fail

In order for believers to live for God well,
They need to be open and willing to fail.
Humbly living all in, with nothing to prove,
With a teachable heart, for the Spirit to move.
The focus can't be on the one who serves,
But on God alone for glory He deserves.

This mindset brings things into perspective,
Then His work can be shown more effective.
When fear of failure begins to blind,
"It's not about me," we must remind.
The focus should always and forever be,
On the Lord alone, His glory to see.

He can be shown, even when we fail,
Going our own way, to no avail.
Sharing with others what occurred,
When our perspective became blurred.
Just a reminder, we can't, but He can,
Gives an opportunity to glorify the I Am.

Believers who desire to live life all in,
Are grateful to be used, aware that they sin.
Knowing they're safe every time they fail,
Confession brings grace, He'll never assail.
Perfection not expected, and is never the goal,
We're free to thrive and learn for He's in control.

Am I now trying to win the approval of men, or of God? Or am I trying to please men? If I were still trying to please men, I would not be a servant of Christ.
—Galatians 1:10

In him and through faith in him we may approach God with freedom and confidence.
—Ephesians 3:12

Which character in the Hall of Faith can I most identify with and why?

_____

_____

_____

_____

_____

_____

_____

_____

_____

What am I afraid to try, and why?

_____

_____

_____

_____

_____

_____

_____

_____

_____

_____

_____

Nineteen

Living on the Fringes

Do you have faith in Christ? Before you answer, read the question again and think what it means to be "in." True faith in Christ is believing what God says—that we are sinners who need a Savior. True faith in Christ is believing He is who He claims to be, the One who took our wrongs upon Himself and the punishment our sins deserve. If you believe this, you have faith in who Christ is, and He has placed His Holy Spirit in you.

True faith doesn't invoke a glib response. If it does, we either don't have true faith or we've grown lukewarm to what Christ has done for us. Christ speaks clearly of what He thinks of lukewarm believers.

> These are the words of the Amen, the faithful and true witness, the ruler of God's creation. I know your deeds, that you are neither cold not hot. I wish you were either one or the other! So, because you are lukewarm—neither cold nor hot—I am about to spit you out of my mouth.
> —Revelation 3:14–16

Why does Christ talk so harshly? Because He loves His own so intensely and needs to show the severity of this way of living for true believers.

Those whom I love I rebuke and discipline. So be earnest, and repent. Here I am! I stand at the door and knock. If anyone hears my voice and opens the door, I will come in and eat with him, and he with me. To him who overcomes, I will give the right to sit with me on my throne, just as I overcame and sat down with my Father on his throne. He who has an ear, let him hear what the Spirit says to the churches.

—Revelation 3:19–22

Sin is serious. It took God's Son's death to save us! By true faith, we've been taken from darkness to light, from the power of Satan to God, and placed among those who are being sanctified (Acts 26:18). By this transaction we've been placed in Christ. Faith hasn't placed us on the fringes of His robe. We've been placed in Him! He proves this by placing His Spirit in us to empower us to live differently. But the Holy Spirit doesn't work on His own volition. We must ask for the Spirit's help. The Spirit is called the Helper for a reason because He helps us live like Christ. On our own we can only live in our natural state as one who sins.

Living on the fringes may appear safe, but it's just the opposite, because it's living outside God's will. Fringe believers are fretful, frustrated, and fatigued. It's a miserable way to live, but it's not permanent unless it's chosen to be. Leaving the fringe to live as we've been called in Christ is to put Him in the middle of everything we do. It is living intentionally for Him, not ourselves.

This kind of living is counter to this world and our nature. We naturally default to our old selves. We're saved but still capable of much sin; we prove our need for our Savior continually. Therefore we need a continual recalibrating of our minds to Christ's.

God is full of grace and is faithful to guide those who desire to live in Christ. We're called to live differently (not perfectly) so Christ may be seen through us. "By this all men will know that you are my disciples, if you love one another" (John 13:35). Jesus said this not for others to be able to identify us but to be drawn to Him through us.

Do you want Christ to replace fret with trust, frustration with freedom, and fatigue with a deeper faith? You'll have to abandon the fringe.

Feet in Two Places

Faith given by God grows deeper the more I learn His way,
To plant my feet in this world and the one I'll see some day.
Created to be His manager, positioned above all creation,
From dust I came with a sinful heart, worthy of obliteration.
Implanted with the image of God, and given belief to trust,
With two feet to stand for the One who created me from dust.

The tricky part is remembering, as a believer I have two places,
The world I see before me, and one coming beyond all graces.
Life is easier to navigate when I stand with a foot in each,
Not by my strength but His alone, His throne always in reach.
Praying to walk in obedience in order to finish the race,
Until home with my Savior, seeing Him face to face.

He gave me faith and set me firm on the Rock of my salvation
Yet how quickly pride can rule if I forget my place and station.
Why would the very Creator choose to value and set me free?
Use one of His mountains and trees to place His Son on Calvary?
My Lord and Redeemer proves Himself faithful and true,
The longer I live in both places, the more I want His view.

When He and truth are my focus, I find my life more stable.
For my feet are planted in both places, knowing my God is able.
Having been given dominion to steward everything He provides,
Given a front-row seat to view His work when I choose to abide.
As His manager I must hold loosely what He places in my hand,
Knowing all has already passed through His, strengthens me to stand.

God brings me into balance when in both places I choose to stand,
He equals my weight when my focus is set on the great I AM.
No matter the situation, whatever suffering comes my way,
Symmetry comes when I choose to gaze vertically and stay.
God's reach is never short, He never tires of repositioning,
Faithful to show me where to stand, whenever I am listening.

> For to me, to live is Christ and to die is gain.
> —Philippians 1:21

> He lifted me out of the slimy pit, out of the mud and mire; He set my feet on a rock and gave me a firm place to stand.
> —Psalm 40:2
>
> But in keeping with his promise we are looking forward to a new heaven and new earth, the home of righteousness. So then, dear friends, since you are looking forward to this, make every effort to be found spotless, blameless and at peace with him.
> —2 Peter 3:13–14

How do I really feel? Fretful, frustrated, and/or fatigued? If so, why?

Do I find my footing more in the world, heaven, or more evenly distributed?

TWENTY

All Things

We're a messy work in progress, and the process can be painful. The pain comes from different sources. Sometimes it's from consequences of our own choices or harm done to us by others. Sometimes it's consequences of the fall.

No matter the source, God promises that nothing will go to waste but "that in all God works for the good of those who love him, who are called according to his purpose" (Rom. 8:28). God isn't calling everything that happens good, right, or godly. Traumatic events we've experienced aren't godly. But God promises He'll work good from them. Whatever ash heap we or others have made, He'll bring beauty from it (Isa. 61:3).

How is this possible? The same One who spoke all things into being out of nothing will continue to accomplish what He's spoken. He's not threatened by our "all things" because "nothing is impossible with God" (Luke 1:37).

This is hard to hear and even harder to accept for those who have either done or experienced horrific acts. Keep in mind, sins aren't good. God isn't saying our sinful acts will become good. He has promised to use them in ways we can't imagine to bring us good.

When the deep hurts overwhelm, we must remember the cross. On that day Jesus was publicly mocked, ridiculed, and flogged. Don't just read glibly over that word flogged. Being flogged not only tore skin, but muscles and tendons. Then Jesus was forced to walk through town carrying the beam on which He would be nailed. It was not over yet. He was stripped bare. He wasn't even allowed to wear His undergarment (the article of clothing worn next to the skin). The soldiers had it and were casting lots to see who would win it.

Crucifixes seen today don't paint an accurate picture of Christ's crucifixion. Psalm 22 and Isaiah 52:14 tell us He was so badly beaten He was unrecognizable as even being human!

Beyond this, His misery would soon intensify beyond imagination as the sky darkened when the sun didn't shine on the One who had created it (Mark 15:33; John 1:3). Innocent of any wrong, He hung in darkness reflecting the blackness of our sins, shame, and guilt poured out on Him (1 Pet. 2:24). The One for whom all things are created experienced our blame as if it belonged to Him (John 1:3; Rom. 11:36).

And He experienced this all alone. The Father He'd talked with for all eternity past was silent—an unfathomable thought. Their eternal, perfect fellowship with each other was no more (Mark 15:34). The Father couldn't be present to affirm the Son, and the Spirit couldn't comfort as the full extent of our deserved wrath rained down on Jesus.

Put yourself in the lives of those who loved Jesus at that time. Can you imagine the horror and hopelessness they must have felt when all this happened? How could good ever come from this? When Goodness died it seemed as though nothing good could ever be again. In that moment, they didn't have what we do, the rest of the story. They didn't understand salvation came from the horror of the cross. They didn't understand a deeper trust and connection would come because Jesus identifies with the extent of our sufferings, even though we'll never be able to fully identify with His. They didn't understand Jesus had to be left to suffer alone so we never would have to.

God calls us to trust Him in the process, invite Him into our suffering, and trust goodness will be produced even when we see no sign of it.

All of Me

I want to give all of me, as You gave all of You.
I want to trust Your plan, by surrendering my will too.
I want to walk through life as Christ did, on His knees,
Seeking what You want, so You can have more of me.

Have Your way Lord, please take control,
Grow my trust in You, the Lover of my soul.
Show me Your holiness more each day
Use it to show me how often I go astray.

Help me be mindful of who you are,
You spoke creation, made every star.
You hold all things together, including me,
You've paid the price to set me free.

Your enemy is mine, now I'm on Your side,
But there's another enemy I forget, it's my pride.
Grow a hatred in me toward the things that You hate,
Draw and fix my eyes on Your character in the wait.

You'll bring good from all that's been done,
Nothing threatens You, the battle's been won.
Please grow my faith in Your promises true,
Work all for good to draw me closer to You.

Therefore, I urge you brothers, in view of God's mercy,
to offer your bodies as living sacrifices, holy and pleasing
to God—this is your spiritual act of worship.
—Romans 12:1

Do your best to present yourself to God as one approved,
a workman who does not need to be ashamed and who
correctly handles the word of truth.
—2 Timothy 2:15

What past situation or relationship do I want to see God redeem?

What part of me or my life do I struggle to give to God?

TWENTY-ONE

Challenge of Change

Who likes change? Most people don't because it feels foreign—that is until we need change. With a readiness for change can come an impatience. When we're ready, we want it immediately. But real change takes time.

Change begins in the mind. We only know what we know, and only do what we are used to doing. We are creatures of habit, and our minds gravitate to what is the usual. Change is hard, but over time those who continue to want change receive the power to change that only God can produce (Isa. 43:19).

Change was hard for the early church as the church of Christ expanded into the Greek communities. In Acts 15, we learn Jewish believers struggled to accept Gentile believers because they didn't have to observe all of the Jewish customs and traditions to be considered true followers of Christ.

For generations Jews had been steeped in practices such as circumcision and refraining from certain foods. It was hard to change this mindset and accept believing Greeks as brothers and sisters in Christ. When the Jewish believers refused to accept the Gentile believers unless they were circumcised, God sent Paul and Barnabas to speak on behalf of the believing Gentiles.

The Jews though weren't the only ones who needed to change their thinking. Worshiping God was very different than worshiping pagan gods. No longer would Gentiles worship by practicing sexual immorality or eating food sacrificed to idols. It took time for Jewish believers to fully accept these Gentiles as fellow believers in Christ. It took watching the apostles accept the Gentiles believers before they too began to accept them. It took time for all of them to look only at what God calls us all to look at, the heart. Through changes of action, the changes of the heart are seen.

Are you ready for change? Do you see changes God is making in your way of thinking? Are you experiencing new actions and desires brought about by the changes He's making? Others will see the change too. If they respond negatively, be patient. They're also having a change of mind.

Those who desire to live a life changed by Christ will experience opposition. Expect it. Seek God through it and wait with Him for others to trust the change is real. Seek out those who also desire for God to change them.

This is what the early church did. They gathered together to pray, have meals, and listen to those teaching God's Word. The early church gathered in fear and faith. Their gathering helped them know they weren't alone. Gathering also encouraged accountability to continue to walk in the way of change.

When we desire to be different and are willing to trust God to bring it about, we're ready for change. When we're willing to do whatever God asks to receive the change, we can expect it. God is faithful to bring it.

The new way will feel weird, foreign, and uncomfortable, because it is (1 Pet. 2:11). God calls us to live as "aliens and strangers in the world" because this world isn't our home. Over time the foreign feeling will be more easily embraced. Especially when we find other "foreigners." Together we can embrace God's desire to change us and encourage one another in the process.

> Therefore, we do not lose heart. Though outwardly we are wasting away, yet inwardly we are being renewed day by day.
> —2 Corinthians 4:16

Faith Changes

Faith changes us, leading to action,
Moving forward, creating traction.
Faith lived out begins to reflect,
Who it is our souls have met.

Things we did before,
Don't satisfy anymore.
We find that where we went,
Unsettles us now and we repent.

Three steps forward, two steps back,
Then with prayer we get back on track.
Given power to say no to sin,
Avoiding pain from falling again.

Over time we begin to grow,
More in love with Jesus to know.
Soon wanting to fan the flame,
Living for Him without shame.

Wanting to work for His Name,
So others can have the same.
If others see Him in us grow,
They may ask and want to know.

Why do we do the things we do?
That's easy, love and gratitude.
So much more God has given,
And more to come for His forgiven.

Faith by itself, if it is not accompanied by action, is dead. But someone will say, "You have faith; I have deeds." Show me your faith without deeds, and I will show you my faith by what I do. You believe that there is one God. Good! Even the demons believe that—and shudder. You foolish man, do you want evidence that faith without deeds is useless? Was not our ancestor Abraham considered righteous for what he did when he offered his son Isaac on the altar? You see that his faith and his actions were working together, and his faith was made complete by what he did.

—James 2:17–22

Do I see God changing me? If so, how?

How am I responding to changes (either good or bad) in others?

TWENTY-TWO

But God

Life is so often not like the movies. You know, the ones that begin with some difficulty or tragedy, then end with everything all wrapped up like a beautiful present with a bow. Our lives, what we experience, don't seem like beautifully wrapped presents, but they are a gift. If today your present is hard to receive, I'm deeply sorry and weep as I write this. In times of deep pain, it's tempting to desire a return policy.

When life feels like this, we must remember the precious words God has sprinkled throughout Scripture—"But God." Before God steps onto the scene, the situation seems hopeless, because it is. Here are a few "but God" moments.

The first of these pivotal moments began right after the fall of man. Adam and Eve had just done the only thing God had told them not to do, and their disobedience ruined everything. "But the LORD God called to the man" (Gen. 3:9). Sin had entered the world, but God immediately came to draw mankind to Himself. He told Adam and Eve He would provide the required remedy for their sin through His Son, the Seed to come.

Out of fear, Abraham had told the king Abimelech of Gerar that his wife Sarah was his sister. The king sent for Sarah and took her as his own. "But God came to Abimelech in a dream one night and said to him, 'You are as good as dead because the woman you have taken; she is a married woman'" (Gen. 20:3). Through the king's encounter with God, not only was Sarah released, Abimelech had a beautiful dialogue with God. God blessed Abimelech because he chose humility; he chose to fear God and released Sarah in obedience. God also kept Abimelech from touching Sarah before he received his dream (Gen. 20:6).

Joseph encountered injustice after injustice that began with his brothers selling him as a slave (Gen. 37:23–28; 39:20). None of Joseph's misery was wasted. God used it to train him for what was ahead (Gen. 41:41). Having experienced what God had done, he told his brothers, the ones who had begun his misery, "You intended to harm me, but God intended it for good to accomplish what is now being done" (Gen. 50:20).

No hopeless situation can compare to when the crucified Jesus lay dead in a tomb. "But God raised Him from the dead, freeing him from the agony of death, because it was impossible for death to keep its hold on him" (Acts 2:24).

Mankind rebelled against Him, "But God demonstrated His own love for us in this: While we were still sinners, Christ died for us" (Rom. 5:8).

My dear sister or brother in Christ, the bow on our gift is coming, is beautiful, and will not disappoint! We just can't see it yet. We can't see all God is doing behind the scenes. We can't imagine how He's going to bring a bow out of the destruction before us.

Until we see the bow that awaits us, may we seek "but God" moments in Scripture. May we ask others to share their own "but God" situations that God turned around. As we hear their stories, may we allow ourselves to feel their hopelessness so we can feel God's glory when He steps onto the scene to do what only He can do.

Believe it or not, we all have "but God" moments. We need only ask Him, and He'll remind us of the ones He has especially gifted us with.

God's Remnant

When life looks hopeless, know God isn't done,
He's not finished with those clinging to the Son.
He's weaving and sewing a beautiful tapestry,
Created out of His remnant, to last all eternity.

Remnant of materials are often cast aside,
But God's remnant[3] are used as they abide.
Satan does his best to eradicate God's own,
But don't forget God is still on His throne.

God protects His remnant, not only to survive,
But through the ages empowers them to thrive.
Building God's army for the Lord's renown,
Despite the Enemy trying to take them down.

Sewing more souls together from every nation,
Into the family of God, ones from every station.
Nothing can rip God's own away, His hold is secure,
He strengthens and binds together, so they can endure.

God did not reject his people, whom he foreknew. Don't you know what the Scripture says in the passage about Elijah—how he appealed to God against Israel: "Lord, they have killed your prophets and torn down your altars; I am the only one left, and they are trying to kill me"? And what was God's answer to him? "I have reserved for myself seven thousand who have not bowed the knee to Baal." So too, at the present time there is a remnant chosen by grace. And if by grace then it is no longer by works; if it were, grace would no longer be grace.
—Romans 11:2–6

---

[3] Those who believe in the promised Savior, Jesus, as Lord.

As I reflect on my life, what "but God" moments do I see?

Who are others God has sewn in my life?

Twenty-Three

God Encourages the Called

Has God called you to do something that seems too difficult or massive? Chances are it is. Don't let that threaten you. Instead let it keep you dependent on the One who has called you. Through this, God stretches our faith as He equips us for what He's called us to do.

We see this same stretching in Scripture. God stretched Moses when He called Moses to lead the Israelites out of Egypt (Ex. 3–4).

We see it again after Moses' death when God called Joshua to become the new leader of the Israelites (Josh. 1). Joshua had been serving alongside Moses as his aide. After Moses' death, God told Joshua it was time for him to lead the Israelites into the land God had promised them.

As God was instructing him, God told Joshua, "Be strong and courageous" three times! Did God see fear in Joshua's heart? Was Joshua afraid the people would refuse to listen to him as they had refused to listen to Moses forty years earlier (Deut. 1:19–40)? Was he remembering the powerful enemy and fortified cities he knew they'd have to conquer (Deut. 1:28)?

Whatever the reason, God saw it necessary to remind Joshua three times to "be strong and courageous." Then God encouraged him through the mouths of his own officers (Josh. 1:16–18). When Joshua was relaying God's instructions to his officers, they made clear to him they'd follow him completely to fulfill what God had instructed them to do. They responded to the orders given by saying, "Whatever you have commanded us, we will do." They further promised to take care of any who rebelled and repeated God's very words to Joshua, "Only be strong and courageous!"

We all need encouragement. Nothing encourages a fearful soul more than speaking aloud God's unchanging character. He is the Creator who spoke nature into existence (Gen. 1; Ps. 33:9). He'll give us creative ways to work when we ask. He created time (Gen. 1:14). Watch Him expand ours as we depend on Him.

He equips the called (Heb. 13:20–21), and encourages the weary and fearful to persevere in His strength (Is. 35:3–4). No matter how daunting the task, lay it before God, acknowledge your fears, and speak the truths known about Him. Watch the fear begin to fade as overwhelming feelings of inadequacy are replaced by the overwhelming awareness of God Almighty!

God often encourages His people with those He's placed in their lives. Others can encourage us to stay the course in challenging times. God has also placed us in their lives to speak words of encouragement to them. When we speak God's truth to someone struggling, we also speak it into our own souls. By this we're both encouraged. That's the power of God's Word.

Who in your life needs encouraging? Who can you turn to remind you of what is true about God when you're struggling or fearful? Share your fears with the Lord and others who are also following the Lord. Then watch Him lead you day by day to "be strong and courageous!"

> Therefore encourage one another and build each other up, just as in fact you are doing.
> —1 Thessalonians 5:11

Everyone Needs a Barnabas[4]

Everyone needs a Barnabas, someone to encourage them in life,
With words that build them up, especially during times of strife.
Encouragers are observers, noticing qualities in others unknown,
Telling them how God's using them, how they've spiritually grown.
It takes time, but not always a lot, only requires a heart's desire,
Knowing even small talk can lead to His purpose much higher.

Sometimes no words are necessary, only needed is an ear,
Eyes tender and empathizing to draw the struggling near.
Feeling safe in their presence, know they're listened to,
Failures receive compassion, knowing no judgment's due.
What's heard isn't the focus, but the soul who's in need,
Valued, loved and created, by the One who came to bleed.

A Barnabas finds it easy to love whomever they greet,
To be a beacon pointing to the Lord any soul they meet.
Either with words or a smile, both can be used by Him,
To build up the tired traveler, wandering this world of sin.
Encouragers too get weary, a Barnabas they also need,
Then they require another, to encourage, and take the lead.

Rewards for the encourager are each soul they get to know,
Learning the heart of others, often getting to watch them grow.
This encourages the encourager to keep encouraging all the more,
They get to see God's handiwork, knowing He has more in store.
Like all who serve the Lord, encouragers willingly sacrifice,
Hearing "Well done, good and faithful," the words of Christ.

---

[4] Barnabas was a man from Cyprus. His given name was Joseph, but the apostles called him Barnabas, which means son of encouragement (Acts 4:36). When Paul was converted, the apostles were afraid to trust him. Barnabas took Paul before the apostles and told them how Paul had spoken boldly about Jesus in Damascus. When many Greeks in Antioch became believers, Barnabas was sent to them. He stayed with them for a year and encouraged them greatly (Acts 11:20–23).

Joseph, a Levite from Cyprus, whom the apostles called Barnabas (which means Son of Encouragement), sold a field he owned and brought the money and put it at the apostles' feet.
—Acts 4:36

The Lord's hand was with them, and a great number of people believed and turned to the Lord. News of this reached the ears of the church at Jerusalem, and they sent Barnabas to Antioch. When he arrived and saw evidence of the grace of God, he was glad and encouraged them all to remain true to the Lord with all their hearts. He was a good man, full of the Holy Spirit and faith, and a great number of people were brought to the Lord.
—Acts 11:21–24

Who has God placed in my life as my encouragers?

Who has He placed in my life who needs encouragement?

TWENTY-FOUR

The Gift of Pain

Thank God for painful consequences to sin. If not for pain, I would stay the same. If not for pain, I would not desire the transformation only God can bring. Painful consequences are a gift from God. I'm not saying I love pain, but I need it. In my flesh, I need bad results to come from my bad choices. If there was not pain from bad choices, I would keep going the same way, seeking my own fleshly desires. Nothing can help us draw closer to God than living in the bad consequences of when we didn't.

In Genesis 32:22–32, we read of Jacob given pain because he refused to surrender. Jacob wrestled with God all night long. Verse 25 tells us, "When the man saw he could not overpower him, he touched Jacob's hip so that his hip was wrenched as he wrestled with him." Jacob wasn't more powerful than God, but God could see Jacob's refusal to yield to Him. Jacob told the Lord he wouldn't let Him go until He blessed him.

God blessed Jacob in two ways. First, God gave him a new name: "Your name will no longer be Jacob but Israel, because you have struggled with God, with men and have overcome" (v. 28). Then God also blessed Jacob with a limp. Both the new name and the limp were reminders of Jacob's refusal to let go.

Scripture doesn't say if Jacob's limp lasted the rest of his life. No matter how long he limped, his new name stuck. And when it was spoken it reminded him not only of his stubborn nature, but God's mercy. Jacob named the place where they had wrestled Peniel, saying, "It is because I saw God face to face and yet my life was spared" (Gen. 32:30).

Nothing can touch our relationship with God if we trust Jesus took our deserved punishment for our wrongs (Rom. 8:29–30; 2 Tim. 2:11–13). God Himself holds our relationship secure and seals us with the Holy Spirit to prove it (2 Cor. 1:21–22). Our refusal to surrender to His way does not affect our relationship but our fellowship with Him.

Any break in our fellowship is immediately mended by repentance. It's not so easy though with others. Our selfness and stubbornness to see things the way we want not only breaks our fellowship with those we love, it can also break our relationship with them. Repentance can mend our relationships, but not always. Forgiveness takes time if they choose to give it.

Are you living in painful consequences from past sins? Let's let the hard consequences remind us of the mercy and grace of God. May they spur us to open His Word and learn more of the One who loves us affectionately, extravagantly, and absolutely. Let's let the pain press us closer to Him in prayer, His Word, and fellowship with others doing the same. The pain is there for a purpose, so let's use it for our good and to point others to Him.

> Therefore, tell the people: This is what the LORD Almighty says: "Return to me," declares the LORD Almighty, "and I will return to you," says the LORD Almighty."
> —Zechariah 1:3
>
> Godly sorrow brings repentance that leads to salvation and leaves no regret, but worldly sorrow brings death.
> —2 Corinthians 7:10

Gift of Pain

If we never felt pain's agony,
From choices even physically.
Imagine touching a stove top,
Never realizing it was hot.
Unaware the damage done,
Sensation to our hand none.
How destroyed we would be,
Harming ourselves repeatedly.

In love God gave the gift of pain,
For without it we'd choose to remain.
Stuck, so numb in our path of misery,
With no desire or hope of being set free.
But pain He gave to lead us to cry out,
Revealing the futility of our choices and doubt.
Praise God, how helpful pain can be,
To lead us to surrender our insanity.

Before I was afflicted I went astray,
but now I obey your word.
—Psalm 119:67

It was good for me to be afflicted so
that I might learn your decrees.
—Psalm 119:71

What has God taught me through past painful consequences?

What would my life look like if God never brought painful consequences to my sins?

TWENTY-FIVE

From Death to Life

Have you ever been present when someone died? I have, and it was hard to accept the person was gone. No more life-sustaining breath, no more life . . . no more.

Our world today can be sterile when it comes to death. Dying commonly takes place in a facility. Those who lose loved ones often aren't present when the last breath is taken. Usually someone else washes and dresses the body and waits for the funeral director.

I know this is a morbid topic, but stay with me.

My dad was at home when we lost him. A few of us were beside him when he took his last breath. After he passed, I kept looking for one more breath as I held his hand. I wasn't ready to lose him. After a while, the hospice nurse and I began to wash and prepare him. We dressed him in a fresh pair of pajamas and positioned his still warm body under the sheet while we waited for the funeral director to arrive.

While waiting, I looked at my dad and began to think of the people we're told about in Scripture who were dead and Christ brought back to life.

I thought to myself, *I can't imagine if Dad began to breathe again, got out of bed, and started making his delicious biscuits and gravy!* My dad loved to cook and feed those he loved. I imagined how those in Scripture must have felt when they saw their dead rise.

One of those Jesus raised was the twelve-year-old daughter of a man named Jairus (Luke 8:40–56). He was a synagogue ruler who came to Jesus, fell at His feet, and begged Him to come and put his hands on his little girl who was dying. Jairus believed Jesus could heal her. Then some men from Jairus' house walked up to Jairus and told him, "Your daughter is dead, don't bother the teacher any more" (v. 49).

Upon hearing this, Jesus told Jairus, "Don't be afraid; just believe and she will be healed" (v. 50). Jesus, along with Peter, James, and John, went with Jairus to his home. When they entered the house, loud mourners were present. Jesus said to them, "She is not dead but asleep."

The mourners laughed at Him as they knew the child was dead. After putting the mourners out, Jesus took the child's parents and the disciples into where the child was.

Then Jesus took the child by the hand and said, "My child, get up!" Immediately the girl's spirit returned, she stood up and walked around. Her parents were completely astonished. Jesus told them give her something to eat and ordered them not to tell anyone what had happened.

Can you imagine seeing the dead begin to breathe and start walking around? And can you imagine having to keep it a secret? No wonder those who witnessed this gave their lives willingly to spread the gospel. They had seen the dead rise and would soon see their Savior do the same. This same resurrection power would be given to them after Christ's ascension (Acts 2).

How quickly we can forget this same resurrection power has been placed in each of us who also believe in Christ as Savior. We can forget we were dead but now alive. We are no longer who we were before He saved us.

When we forget, we go back to dead behavior that destroys our peace. May we remember His words are for us too, "Don't be afraid; just believe." When we cling to His words of life, He empowers us to say no to our old dead way of living. He has cleaned us in His blood and dressed us in His robes of righteousness. And He has told us not to keep it a secret but to testify to those we encounter, telling them who He is and what He's done.

Death Removed to Die

Death's been removed from us since Christ paid the price,
Born again, made imperishable because of His sacrifice.
Chosen before all creation, we were on the mind of God,
Known fully, loved affectionately, even though flawed.

Death can be within us still, when we daily choose,
To give over and kill our will, winning when we lose.
This kind of death produces sincere love from the heart,
Spirit-fueled thoughts and actions, to live set apart.

Death to the empty way of life handed down to us,
Now real living can happen when we choose to trust.
As we set our hope upon the One who gives grace,
Dying to self for obedience, wanting to finish our race.

Death to worry must happen, what others think of us,
Whose opinion we value most, reveals in whom we trust.
When Christ is our focus, abundant living comes into view,
This kind of living is easier when companions die to self too.

Death like this is possible within believers every day,
Death to self is required for those walking the Narrow Way.
This kind of death brings freedom to live like never before,
Giving a taste of their eternal life, all that He has in store.

Therefore, do not let sin reign in your mortal body so that you obey its evil desires. Do not offer the parts of your body to sin, as instruments of wickedness, but rather offer yourselves to God, as those who have been brought from death to life; and offer the parts of your body to him as instruments of righteousness. For sin shall not be your master, because you are not under law, but under grace.

—Romans 6:12–14

I have been crucified with Christ and I no longer live, but Christ lives in me. The life I live in the body, I live by faith in the Son of God, who loved me and gave himself for me.

—Galatians 2:20

What sinful pattern in my life needs to die?

Who can I ask to pray for me to have God's power to say no and hold me accountable?

Twenty-Six

Stay in Your Own Lane

Imagine driving down the road and a car beside you begins to drift into your lane, forcing you to swerve. You've gone from minding your own business to being unsure if you can trust this driver to stay in his lane. Oblivious to his drifting, the driver switches to your lane and keeps on driving.

That's what happens when someone tries to dictate your choices. It's hard for him to stay in his lane when his eyes are focused on your path, not his own. When he begins to drift over, just give a gentle tap on your horn, letting him know he's swerved into your lane. If he ignores the horn, and continues to cross the boundary with a blatant lack of desire to learn, distance is needed.

The person may ask, "Why the distance?" If so, lovingly tell him what warranted it. He may be willing to quit swerving and ask for a horn tap while he's learning the new skill of staying in his lane.

Do you find yourself being the one swerving? You may be thinking, *Isn't it wrong to stay silent?* After all, Colossians 3:16 instructs us to "teach and admonish one another with all wisdom." Aren't we called to guide, correct, and direct those we love? Yes, when we're called to do so, but by the Spirit, not out of fear or frustration.

Scripture also instructs in 1 Thessalonians 4:11 "to mind your own business." How do we know when to instruct, admonish, or mind our own business? Only God knows! Therefore it's our job to keep asking Him. Until then, we are to stay in our own lane (Prov. 2:6).

Staying in our own lane is hard when we love others deeply. It's especially hard when their misery becomes our misery. I've found what to do next depends on the kind of misery I'm experiencing.

The mistakes of others may make us miserable emotionally, tempting us to try to fix their problems for them. But this isn't loving them. Love is selfless action for another's best interest. When they're experiencing hard consequences from bad decisions made, removing their consequences isn't loving them. Giving unsolicited advice in hopes they'll follow it and put an end to our mutual misery isn't loving them.

When someone's lane is more the focus than our own, it's best to take the first exit into a rest stop to meditate on who God is. When those we love go off the rails, God isn't in a panic. He's sovereign, not a follower. He's omnipotent, not impotent. He is not only capable but also promises in all things He works for the good of those who love Him (Rom. 8:28). He's holding all things together, and that includes them, you, and me (Col. 1:17). He alone knows what's best. No matter what happens, nothing will be wasted. All will be used.

Each poor choice builds a dissatisfaction. With enough poor choices, the miserable grow weary and are ready for change. I've found this in my own life. It took a lot of misery for me to finally be willing to surrender in situations. Misery can lead unbelievers to salvation and believers to trust God in the messiness of the Narrow Road.

Are you miserable enough from doing the same thing and expecting a better outcome than last time? Are you weary from all of the swerving?

Change begins in the mind. God will begin to change us when we're ready to focus on our own lane. The longer we stay in our own lane, the more energy we'll find we have. It takes a lot more fuel to swerve.

What Plank?

Have you, like me, ever had a plank in your eye?
Focusing on another's sin, while your own you deny?
There are many whys behind the choices that are made,
Like a whitewashed Pharisee, I've judged instead of prayed.
From my ivory tower I've thought I was discerning what is true,
Oblivious to the distortion by the plank in my view.

I can't remember life before a plank was in my eye,
Thinking I'm better than others and feeding that lie.
Whacking others with my plank as I turned around,
Smugly wondering why they were on the ground,
God began to show me the ugliness of this wrong,
Making clear, in His children, it does not belong.

For the plank to be removed the Father must assist,
He's as gentle as possible, so I'll trust and not resist.
Since then, I've met others with a plank like me,
It's hard not to run away and avoid their company.
So much is not seen when there's a plank in your eye,
The pain it causes relationships only God can rectify.

Thankfully, once the plank is plucked from its dwelling place,
God exposes even more sins, each one covered by grace.
It's precious to see the acceptance others have given me,
Loving me right where I am, not where I want to be.
Pride seems to be my thorn, so another plank can form,
Humble self, confess often, and read Scripture to conform.

Over time God is helping me to give what I've been given,
Grace and mercy, not a critical look, to forgive as I'm forgiven.
To pray for those quick to judge, God is who convicts and tells,
Have compassion knowing the longer there, the more it swells.
If ever they become willing to see and want it to be removed,
They'll find He's as gentle as possible, and their sight improved.

> Why do you look at the speck of sawdust in your brother's eye and pay no attention to the plank in your own eye? How can you say to your brother, "Let me take the speck out of your eye," when all the time there is a plank in your own eye? You hypocrite, first take the plank out of your own eye, and then you will see clearly to remove the speck from your brother's eye.
> —Matthew 7:3–5

Do I have a tendency to be the one swerving or being swerved into?

What plank do I need to see?

Twenty-Seven

Call of the Common

God's servants are often unimportant in the world's eyes. We find this in Scripture as well as in ministries today. Those who are quiet, unimpressive, dismissed, lacking in confidence or education by the world's standards are often the ones God selects.

He encourages us with example after example throughout the Bible. He also tells us, "Do not despise meager beginnings" (Zech. 4:10 NLT). Our background, status, opportunity or lack of, is purposeful. God is orchestrating and molding us for the grand plan He has ahead of those who answer His call.

There is a beautiful result that comes out of God choosing the lowly—He alone shines. It's His powerful transformation of them that gets others' attention.

Take the Samaritan woman at the well (John 4:1–42). We don't even know her name, but we know her story. We see her transformation from one of shame, avoiding others by coming to the well in the heat of the day to one of joyfully running to bring others to Jesus.

Then there's the apostle Peter, an unschooled, ordinary man who was used in one occasion to speak to a crowd, and about three thousand of them became believers (Acts 2:41). Later, Peter spoke to the Sanhedrin, a group of highly educated men who served under the high priest. They were astonished by him and "took note these men had been with Jesus" (Acts 4:13).

God continues to use the common today. Many thriving ministries have been started by just a few souls hungry for the Word of God. Bible Study Fellowship, a ministry that can be found all over the world, was started by five women wanting to learn the Bible and one willing to teach them. The Navigators, another worldwide ministry, was started by one worker at a lumberyard teaching a fellow believer how to live for Christ.

It doesn't take a keen mind or confidence but one who is "humble and contrite in spirit and trembles at my word" (Isa. 66:2). If our confidence is in ourselves, it'll only get in the way of what God wants to accomplish through us. God's ministries require a soul sold out for Christ, one who remembers his neediness and is willing to be surrendered to God and follow His direction. Confidence will grow, not in ourselves, but in the One who has made the ministry possible.

Is God laying something on your heart? Do you feel ill-equipped? Good! That's where He wants us to be and stay. Ask Him what He wants you to do. Plan to be patient while He puts all the pieces into place. Ask Him what to do while you're waiting. Ask Him to bring others alongside who are feeling the same call. God is faithful. He will bring about all He has planned. Those who continue to follow His leading will get to play a part. By this they will have a front- row seat to watch and experience what only God can do.

> But God chose the foolish things of the world to shame the wise; God chose the weak things of the world to shame the strong. He chose the lowly things of the world and the despised things—and the things that are not—to nullify the things that are, so that no one may boast before him. It is because of him that you are in Christ Jesus, who has become for us wisdom from God—that is, our righteousness, holiness, and redemption. Therefore, as it is written: "Let him who boasts boast in the Lord."
> —1 Corinthians 1:27–31

A Successful Life

How we define success determines a satisfied life,
Success can still exist even during dark times and strife.
This is only possible because of the Source that brings,
The satisfaction to our soul when Christ is everything.

When our desire is to seek His will, then we will find,
Him faithfully beginning to slowly transform our mind.
We'll begin to see things more from His point of view,
Trusting in the process and His power to pull us through.

A longing will grow in us to want to seek His way,
A pattern will grow in us to hit our knees and pray.
A desire will grow in us for Him to rule and reign.
A trust will grow in us that He'll use even our pain.

Having our own agenda will no longer be our goal,
But to grow His Kingdom, praying for one more soul.
All done through His power, resting while we work,
Fueled by what He's doing with no desire to shirk.

How we once measured success soon cannot be found,
Seeking God's definition keeps us on solid ground.
Money loses its enticement, desire for fame fades away,
His success is our desire, fully satisfied in His way.

The poor will eat and be satisfied; those
who seek the LORD will praise him!
—Psalm 22:26

Delight yourself in the LORD, and he
will give you the desires of your heart.
—Psalm 37:4

What is God calling me to do?

How does God define success differently than the world?

Twenty-Eight

Chain Breaker

Have you ever been to the circus? If so, you've seen elephants doing tricks. Have you wondered how trainers gain control over these powerful animals? I've been told they begin when the elephant is a baby by placing a heavy chain around one of its legs. Naturally, the baby elephant tries to pull and tug at the chain, but to no avail. No matter how hard it tries, it can't snap the chain. After continuous attempts to free itself, it stops trying. After a while, the trainer removes the chain. The elephant is so accustomed to the chain, it thinks it's still there. By this time though it has grown in size and strength and could easily overpower the trainer. With just one swipe of its trunk, it could throw its trainer to the ground—that is if it knew it was free.

As believers we often live our lives like these elephants when we try to rid ourselves of a destructive habit to no avail. We're either blinded by pride as we deny our helplessness or don't yet know how to live in the freedom Christ has purchased for us.

It's not hopeless for us to change. What's hopeless is that we can bring it about on our own. Salvation and sanctification are both God's work. Salvation means we've been freed from sin's power to rule and reign over us (Rom. 3:12; 6:14). We've been given a new heart and a new spirit (Ezekiel 36:26). Our flesh and this world will tempt us to trust our thinking and ideas of how to change instead of asking God what to do (Isa. 55:8; 1 John 2).

Satan wants us to feel bound in the shame of past sins, hopeless that we'll ever change, and fearful of the future. The devil wants us discouraged, hoping we'll keep trying to rely on our own strength, because this only increases our misery. He also knows what it takes for us to see change.

If we acknowledge we're as weak as a baby elephant chained to a pole, we can surrender to God and allow the Holy Spirit to work in us. God is patient, persistent, and always forgiving. God isn't like an elephant trainer. He's set us free from the wrath our sins deserve, set us free from sin's power to rule and reign in our hearts, and promised us eternity in heaven free of sin's presence. This side of heaven, God promises to walk with us all the way and to keep reminding us we're free.

What shackles do you "think" you are wearing? Have you tried to stop a bad habit only to find you've picked up a different one? This is what happens when we try to stop in our own power.

Are you living with hard consequences from past sins? The consequences don't come with chains. We're still free to walk with the Chain Breaker. God never gives up on us. He knows we're a messy work in process.

Tell another believer what has you in bondage and ask for prayer. Preach the gospel to your soul, and remember God's placed His resurrection power in you. All it takes for God to unleash the Holy Spirit's power is for you to ask.

Are you ready to be set free? Ask God to show you how to live this way and keep asking Him one day at a time, one moment at a time. He's faithful, and promises to give His strength to those embracing their weakness. "My grace is sufficient for you, for my power is made perfect in weakness" (2 Cor. 12:9). Then we'll get a taste of the freedom He's already given.

> If the Son sets you free, you will be free indeed.
> —John 8:36

Chain Breaker

Sin's tug of temptation can feel like that old chain,
Escape is futile when bound to the old life to claim.
Then shame and disgrace will grow in the heart,
Forgetting with faith in Christ these have no part.
When sin's chain was broken, so was its shame,
Disgrace and dishonor can't hold or reclaim.

Much transpired the day our sin's chain was broken,
When God gave faith to believe what He had spoken.
Sin lost the ability to take captive and hold,
It must be given permission to bind and mold.
The presence of sin is all that the devil has left,
Cling to the Chain Breaker, dwell in His cleft.

> Then they cried to the LORD in their trouble, and he saved them out of their distress. He brought them out of darkness and the shadow of death, and broke their chains in pieces. Oh, that men would give thanks to the LORD for his goodness and to his wonderful works to the children of men!
> —Psalm 107:13–15 NKJV

What am I tempted to do when things don't go the way I hope?

Will I ask God to empower me to live differently than before?

Twenty-Nine

Last Words

*I*magine if you knew today was your last day to live. What would your last words be to those you love?

As Christ gathered with His disciples the night before He died, He had many words for those faithful to Him. Jesus had already dismissed His betrayer Judas with the chilling words, "What you are about to do, do quickly" (John 13:27). Jesus knew Judas only pretended to love Him.

Then Jesus spoke to those who really did. Much responsibility rode on the backs of these eleven men. They were the ones God chose to carry out Christ's mission, share what He'd done, and begin His church. Jesus told them their obedience would be what stood them apart from the world.

He said, "By this all men will know that you are my disciples, if you love one another" (John 13:35). "If you love me, you will obey what I command" (John 14:15). "Anyone who has my commands and obeys them, he is the one who loves me" (John 14:21). "If anyone loves me, he will obey my teaching" (John 14:23). "If you obey my commands, you will remain in my love" (John 15:10). "Greater love has no one than this, that he lay down his life for his friends. You are my friends if you do what I command" (John 15:13–14).

Do you see a pattern? Love isn't a feeling but an action. Jesus showed what love is by not treating Judas any differently than the other disciples when he washed his feet (John 13:1–17). Jesus showed love for the Father by wanting to be "about the Father's business" (Luke 2:49 KJV).

Love is sacrificing our will for the Father's (Mark 14:36). Love is forgiving (Luke 23:34). Love is giving up our rights. Jesus, Creator and Lord, did this for us by coming as a helpless babe (Phil. 2:7). His final act of love was the cross, fulfilling John 3:16. "God so loved the world" in this way.

Does obedience come hard for you? Does it seem like a drudgery or obligation to do what God commands? If so, legalism has slipped into love's place. When our motive to obey is out of how others will see us or how we see ourselves, pride has blinded us from the sight of the cross.

Legalism produces a rigid and strict mindset to do what's right, while love produces a free and grateful mindset. Legalism is exhausting, because we're working in our own strength, not allowing God to work through us (Heb. 13:20–21). Legalism keeps us from worship because we can't worship when we're self-focused. Real worship flows freely when we're captivated by Jesus. Obeying won't be our focus when we're too busy being captivated by Him. His love will spill out of us onto others. We'll even find God giving us love for those hard to love, knowing someone probably finds us hard to love.

Only God knows the date of our death. Most of us won't have the opportunity to give last words to those we love. But we can choose to love with our lives. Words of love are empty if they aren't backed by action.

How well we love others reflects whom we really love most. We can't love perfectly like Christ. We're going to make mistakes. When we do, we can still choose to love others by asking forgiveness and making amends, when possible. God's version of love looks different from what the world considers to be love. That's why it stands out when it occurs. Each day we have numerous opportunities to love others by our actions. Whom do our actions show we love more—our Savior or ourselves?

Love on Display

True love is something seen, its actions on display,
Fruit of the Spirit, given to the pliable who pray.
Love isn't of this world, so when seen it stands apart,
Drawing others to the light of Christ, shining within the heart.
Love is patient, love is kind, it's mercy, not judgment deserved,
Doesn't envy what another has, grateful for them, God reserved.

It's not proud, so no thought of boasting, not lacking manners or rude,
Nor self-protecting, remember Christ was willing to be crucified nude.
Love isn't easily angered, takes much to offend those with a long fuse,
Keeps no record of wrongs, knowing those who hold grudges only lose.
Love doesn't delight in evil for truth is what brings delight and joy,
Love protects, trusts, hopes, and perseveres, though evil tries to destroy.

This world says love is a feeling, warm and fuzzy, but it's so much more,
Love is God, who gives extravagantly, and has so much more in store.
When we seek to love like God does, when we're captivated by Him,
He empowers us to love like Christ, and to turn away from sin.
One day we'll see the face of our Savior, and the love in His eyes,
Till then may He love others well through us, till our own demise.

Love is patient, love is kind. It does not envy, it does not boast, it is not proud. It is not rude, it is not self-seeking, it is not easily angered, it keeps no record of wrongs. Love does not delight in evil but rejoices with the truth. It always protects, always trusts, always hopes, always perseveres. Love never fails. But where there are prophecies, they will cease; where there are tongues, they will be stilled; where there is knowledge, it will pass away. . . Now we see but a poor reflection as in a mirror; then we shall see face to face. Now I know in part; then I shall know fully, even as I am fully known. And now these three remain: faith, hope and love. But the greatest of these is love.

—1 Corinthians 13:4–8, 12–13

Who or what do I think about throughout the day?

How do I respond to God's Word in action and attitude?

Thirty

Hard to Watch

It's hard to watch someone suffer verbal abuse. I'm not talking about a rare careless word thrown in anger. Abusers are more sinister. Their words are intentional to wound and emotionally beat down another to gain or regain control over them.

If you have known someone who has been emotionally abused, you've seen suffering that only God can heal. Often a professional counselor is needed in the healing process. The pain goes deep and takes much time and effort to heal.

Verbal abuse should never be taken lightly. I learned this after two women very close to me suffered verbal abuse. Each one, at different times, spent a night at our home because she was fearful of her husband. Each wife hadn't told her husband where she was going. When his wife didn't return home that night, a safe husband would have been worried. But both of these husbands only proved their evil intent by blowing up their phones with threatening messages.

One of them, upon finding where his wife was staying, slit all four of her tires. The other husband texted that he'd send his motorcycle gang out to find her.

Those of you who haven't been threatened by someone this unsafe may be thinking as I did, *Run for the hills!* And that's what we did. Both were taken to a safe place until further actions could be taken for their protection. Today both of these women thankfully are free from their abusers, but their scars still remain.

The helpless feeling of watching these women suffer reminds me of Luke who was with Paul on many of his journeys (Acts 28:1; 2 Tim. 4:11). Luke was a physician who could take care of Paul physically (Col. 4:14). As Paul traveled to preach of Christ, many didn't want to hear about Jesus, and some responded with violence.

In Acts 14:19 we read Paul was stoned, dragged out of the city, and left for dead. In Acts 16:22–23, we see Paul and Silas were stripped, beaten, and then severely flogged. In 2 Timothy 4:14, Paul shares, "Alexander the metalworker did a great deal of harm to me." Thankfully, at these events and others, Luke was present to stitch him up, perhaps set his bones, and try to bring comfort to his battered brother in Christ. In Colossians 4:11–14, Paul speaks of his dear friends with him, Luke being one of them, saying they "have proved a comfort to me."

Just imagine the heaviness of Luke's heart as he tended to Paul's wounds. Did resentment build toward the many who inflicted Paul with such senseless pain? Was Luke stricken with fear each time they entered a town? He doesn't say. In much of Acts, Luke is a silent writer, but periodically we're reminded of his presence when he writes "we." In Acts 28, we see Luke too suffered physically. Still traveling with Paul when Paul was imprisoned, he went without food for fourteen days. He nearly lost his life and was shipwrecked (Acts 27:27–28:1).

Close companions of the abused sometimes experience what the abused experience regularly. We too may have hurtful words flung at us when trying to help the abused. The closer we are to those suffering, the harder it is to watch.

How we respond is up to us. If we let our own anger grow toward the abuser, we'll end up trying to take matters into our own hands and make a bad situation worse. If we let fear and the "what ifs" consume us, we'll be of no use to help the abused. Instead, we need to ground ourselves in truth, pray often, and seek God as well as professionals for guidance. We also need to pray for the power to forgive the abuser. By this, we'll be steady to sit with them in their suffering and when necessary help them flee when they're ready.

God's Comfort, His Sovereignty

Take comfort, God throughout history,
Continues to prove His sovereignty,
No matter how dark it seems,
God is working behind the scenes.

Keeps His promises, every one,
Consider each as good as done.
Depend on God, He controls all,
Providing strength for His call.

Seen in Scripture over and over again,
No matter the enemy, God always wins.
Pharaoh's men chased Israelites down,
Only in the Red Sea to drown.

Five kings of Amorites attacked Israel,
But God aided Israel and hailstones killed.
Haman built gallows high,
For himself, not Mordecai.

Herod planned to take Peter down,
Yet he was killed by worms found.
Remember these and others too,
When life looks hopeless to you.

God has a plan we can't yet see,
Cling to His sure sovereignty.
This side of heaven we can't understand,
But we can fully trust, God is in command.

Remember the former things, those of long ago; I am God, and there is no other; I am God, and there is none like me. I make known the end from the beginning from ancient times, what is still to come. I say: My purpose will stand and I will do all that I please. From the east I summon a bird of prey; from a far-off land, a man to fulfill my purpose. What I have said, that will I bring about; what I have planned, that will I do.

—Isaiah 46:9–11

How do I respond to another's suffering?

How does trusting God's sovereignty change my attitude and behavior?

THIRTY-ONE

The Lonely

Are you lonely? Do you feel like no one really understands your struggle? As believers, we know God's there with us, but feelings of loneliness can still overwhelm. It can sometimes seem as if no one cares or is available.

No matter how we feel, there's always One who understands—Jesus. He alone feels our pain more than we'll ever know. But the same can't be said for us. No one knows loneliness like Jesus, no one. When He came in the flesh, He made Himself alone for us. When feeling all alone, we have One who knows.

You might be thinking, *But Jesus is God, how hard could His loneliness really have been?* To answer this, we must understand the degree to which Jesus loves. He loves deeper than we ever will. He cares more than we ever will. He desires a connection with His own like we never will. He wants to connect with us no matter how many times we take Him for granted.

Because of His great love for us and His Father, He came to make Himself vulnerable, and to give us the eternal connection we needed with the Father. He understands our suffering. He knows the feeling of not being understood. He knows what it's like to be unwanted and rejected by the very ones He created. He knows what it's like to be abandoned by those He loves, just when He needed them most. All of this shows His suffering to be exponentially greater than ours.

While Jesus was on earth, His siblings didn't believe He was the Son of God (John 7:5). His family didn't understand Him, and at least at one time thought He was crazy (Mark 3:20–21). Peter, the one whom He would call to lead His apostles, would deny even knowing Him (Luke 22:54–61). Knowing this would happen didn't lessen the pain of emotional abandonment.

Before this occurred, when Christ was in deep sorrow to the point of death and desperate for companionship, He didn't find it (Matt. 26:36–45). It wasn't because He didn't ask, He did. They were willing but unable, due to fatigue. Those closest to Jesus (Peter, James, and John) were unable to sit in the pit of despair with Him. They didn't understand what Jesus was going through.

Their willingness may have comforted Jesus but it couldn't have lessened the weight of what was coming. Everything pales in comparison to the depth of loneliness Christ faced on the cross. He wasn't a bystander when the full extent of our disgrace, guilt, and wrath—not His own—was put on Jesus (2 Cor. 5:21). He didn't feel it for us, He felt it as us. He who knew no sin felt the intensity and horror of shame and guilt consume Him. He felt like a sinner for hours, not just for a moment! He did all of this completely alone. Jesus cried out to the Father, but God couldn't respond. Jesus couldn't be comforted by the Spirit. He had lost connection with the only Ones who had always fully understood Him. His loneliness was unparalleled.

In our loneliness, we are not alone. Jesus is with us, and He's the very best one we could ever ask for. He gets us when no one else does. He'll never leave us but will stay with us all the way—until we see Him face to face. Then we'll see the eyes of the One who sat with us, wept with us, and held us together.

The Loneliest

There is a loneliness that only the Trinity knows,
Occurring days before the Lord Jesus arose.
A plan arranged before the world began,
Because of God's great love for man.
When perfect Jesus took on our sin,
The Holy had to turn away from Him.
For eternity past, One in essence,
This day Jesus banished from their presence.

As innocent Christ took on our wrath,
God accepting Him on our behalf.
The Holy Spirit holds back His power,
No consoling Comforter in this hour.
Unmatched loneliness for the Trinity,
All to give sinners access to divinity.
Even in loneliness, the Trinity perfectly unified,
When upon the cross, God's Son was crucified.

Jesus cried out in a loud voice "My God,
My God, why have you forsaken me."
—Mark 15:34

God has said, "Never will I leave you;
never will I forsake you."
—Hebrews 13:5

What do I do when I'm lonely?

Is loneliness a choice?

Thirty-Two

In the Cleft

One night we had a storm where we live in Oklahoma, and it was fierce. I figured we'd had a tornado, but later found out the damage was caused by 150 mile-an-hour gale-force wind. The next day I was surprised to see all the damage in our neighborhood. Trees were down and one fallen tree had a root ball more than five feet high. We had no damage, not even a fallen limb.

I thought of the words from Fanny Crosby's well-known gospel song, "He hideth my soul in the cleft of the rock . . . and covers me there with His hand" (see Exod. 33:21–22).

The storm was a visual of what was happening in our hearts. Our family was fractured, and putting us back together seemed hopeless. All of us were at fault, but none of us yet understood our own part. During the storm, my husband and I had both woken up, heard the howling wind, and rolled over to go back to sleep. We were unaware we each had done the same until we spoke the next morning. Our hearts were so broken that we didn't care if the storm took us.

Hopelessness is palpable. It consumes the one hopeless. Believers aren't immune from it—no one is. As believers, we know our eternal life stands firm because of Christ. But when life hurts most, how do we live in the now?

Through pain God has taught me it helps to walk through suffering like Christ did in the garden and on the cross.

Jesus prayed and asked those closest to Him to pray (Matt. 26:36–43). Jesus knew what was coming, and He knew intimacy with the Father was vital. Stay close in prayer.

Jesus asked His Father to forgive those who put Him on the cross (Luke 23:34). Jesus' heart was tender toward those killing Him. A hard heart refuses to forgive and seeks vindication (Heb. 3:8). God won't work in a heart bent on bitterness (Eph. 4:17–19, 31–32). Unlike Christ, when someone has sinned against us, oftentimes we've also sinned against them. If we ask God, He'll show us our part.

Jesus took care of others (John 19:26–27). Looking down at His mother and John, He gave them both someone to love. After Jesus died, they could grieve together and take care of each other the way they wanted to take care of Jesus. Grieve with others also grieving, and love others by serving.

Jesus welcomed the repentant thief into His forever family. Both thieves had hurled insults, but when one of them was convicted, believed Jesus, and asked to be a part of His kingdom, he was welcomed (Matt. 27:44; Luke 23:43). May we repent quickly and welcome others who do.

Jesus did as He always had, cried out to His heavenly Father even when God was silent (Matt. 27:46). God was silent because Jesus was taking on our sins and our wrath; our sin separated Him from the Father. Because of this, we're never separated from God.

Sometimes it can feel that way when we don't see our prayers answered the way we want. Living can be unbearable, but when it is, God will pull us through as we plant ourselves in the cleft of our Rock, knowing He's covering us with His hand.

Today I'm so grateful that part of our family is reconciled! It's beautiful to see the work God has done in us to make this possible. My hope is that we will all be reconciled soon. Until then in God's strength, I'm taking it one day at a time.

Are you in the middle of a storm? Take cover in the cleft of the Rock.

Grieving Together[5]

Mephibosheth's inheritance had already been set,
Provision coming from a man he had never met.
Not only given land, but a purpose in life,
Though crippled, he could now provide for his kids and wife.

David gave so much to this man with broken feet,
Much more than a place at the king's table to eat.
For the king had loved his dad more than a brother,
Now they could share stories of Jonathan with each other.

Grieving is best done with others who also miss them,
Those who knew them well, the good, ugly, victories, and sin.
Learning even more about them from another's point of view,
And hearing their name again from someone other than you.

The sharing of their memory not only brings laughter and tears,
But the love that others have for them seems to bring them near.
Their life forever treasured, so grateful to have known them,
And if in God's family, the joy of seeing them again.

> And now, dear brothers and sisters, we want
> you to know what will happen to the believers
> who have died so you will not grieve like people
> who have no hope. For since we believe that
> Jesus died and was raised to life again, we also
> believe that when Jesus returns, God will bring
> back with him the believers who have died.
> —1 Thessalonians 4:13–14 NLT

---

[5] From the events in 2 Samuel 9.

How do I respond to the storms of life?

What are the benefits of grieving with others grieving?

THIRTY-THREE

Waiting Well

Who likes to wait? Throughout our day we're forced to over and over again. We wait for things as trivial as a tea kettle to whistle or traffic light to change. Some of us are waiting for a difficult situation or relationship to change.

What are we doing in the waiting? We're passing the time with something, on our phones, daydreaming, and if we're honest, often scowling. Waiting is hard. By nature, we're impatient. This microwave, Google, Amazon society only increases an intolerance for waiting.

We're waiting for things out of our control. Time waiting isn't wasted if we allow what God wants to produce through it. With whom we wait is up to us.

Here's an acrostic of four ways we can wait.

W is for Worship

We can worship. Yes, worship even when suffering. There's purpose in the waiting, and God will bring about change even if it's only in us. No matter what a situation looks like, God is still working even when we can't see it. He's working all things, good and bad, for good for those who love Him and have been called according to His purpose (Rom. 8:28). He promises it! The darker the time of waiting, the more dire is our need of worship—to sing to the One who sings over us (Zeph. 3:17).

A is for Assured

We can rest assured God is who He claims to be and we are who He says we are. To find His rest we need to preach the gospel to ourselves—even more so when we're weary from waiting. We are His (John 1:12), loved (John 3:16), forgiven (Eph. 1:7), and created for a purpose (Jer. 29:11). The list of who He says we are in Him is exhaustive, so when exhausted look to the One who refreshes the weary soul (Matt. 11:28).

I is for Identifies

We can remember Christ identifies with us. He knows waiting like no other. He waited thousands of years to come in the flesh to fulfill God's promise (Gen. 3:15). He's been waiting the longest of all to fulfill God's promise to come again (John 14:3).

T is for Testimony

While we wait, we're writing a testimony to others. Those who trust His will and His way are leaving a legacy for the ones who follow. In the waiting we need to ask for His perspective, for Him to empower us with patience, and for Him to show us how to wait to be used for His glory. He'll enable us to live differently than the world while we wait. We need only to ask Him.

Our testimony won't be perfect. We're fallen. We'll fail to trust Him over and over again, but returning to Him only proves our testimony is real. It reveals to both unbelievers and believers alike a testimony of His endless grace, mercy, and power to trust again. Those who don't know Christ may ask how it is we can keep going. How do we have joy and peace when frustration and fatigue should overcome us? Our testimony can also encourage others in Christ to persevere.

Waiting is inevitable but gives opportunity to reflect the One who has been waiting the longest. How we wait is up to us. We can choose to grumble or worship, be short-tempered, or turn to something to distract us in our struggle (worry, overeating, pornography).

Or we can meditate on His promises, resting assured God is still all He claims to be. Remember, Christ identifies with us. Jesus never tried to rush God's plan but gave Himself over to His Father's will.

Christ left a perfect testimony. We all leave a testimony. Others are watching and learning from us. Look for those waiting well and join them. God promises those who choose to wait with Him will become more like Him (John 15).

Wait

There is a word that I often hate,
It is the four-letter word *wait.*
Being a doer who gets things done,
How hard it is to be still with the One.
If I could only see from His point of view,
I'd more often trust Him—faithful and true.
But faith that must see is no faith at all,
True faith trusts and answers His call.

Only God can make a sinner His own,
And promises never to leave us alone.
He can surely handle the mess I'm in,
Using my failures for His glory and win.
God alone knows how, what, and when,
Using challenges to bring me closer to Him.
Yet, when in impatience, I become rushed,
Increasing my suffering, my inner peace crushed.

How I need to trust in that little word *wait,*
For He knows best and His timing's never late.
His way is always better and so far beyond,
What He accomplishes strengthens our bond.
So next time I allow concern to turn into fear,
I need to just wait, for my Savior is near.
His plan is perfect and always brings rest,
Faith is strengthened when put to the test.

Waiting can be the best place to be,
When I wait with the One who set me free.
Learning to rest with the One who is good,
Waiting together for all to be as it should.
Having waited the very longest of all,
Well before creation and before the fall.
May I wait with the longsuffering One,
Till falling at His feet when all waiting is done.

Wait for the Lord; be
strong and take heart and
wait for the Lord.
—Psalm 27:14

For what am I waiting?

How am I waiting?

THIRTY-FOUR

Need Wisdom? Just Ask

What a lavishly generous God we have. Continually, He's pouring out His goodness, mercy, and grace. Throughout the day it's impossible for us to be fully aware of all He's doing for us. With compassion God sees all our troubles, struggles, and fears. With patience God waits for us to turn to Him and seek His presence so He may comfort and provide. God longs for us to ask for His wisdom.

Why does He do all this? So He can give more of Himself. Isn't it mind-blowing how God, who is all-powerful, worthy of complete obedience and loyalty, chooses to love us this way? Even in heaven, we may never be able to grasp why He loves us so. One thing we do know, He'll never stop. God loves to share all He is, and all we need to do to receive is ask.

I've found in my own life, if God has held back, He has had good reason. What seemed like years of unanswered prayers (in my marriage and children) wasn't Him holding back His goodness.

The reasons for our struggles required a stronger faith to bear the truth. The years of waiting were drawing me closer to God. I'd only seen the results of our choices, not the "whys" God alone knew. It seems as though God chooses not to work until I'm worn out enough from a situation to let go of control, or should I say, the illusion of control. In trying to control a situation, I've prayed my agenda, the rigid expectations of what I think needs to happen. Not until I'm at the end of myself, after trying to do things my way, am I willing to get out of God's way so He can work.

God gives lavishly and doesn't hold back anything good, not even His wisdom. But God, being a perfect steward, won't waste it. He doesn't give wisdom to the unwilling, but those ready and willing to follow in humility (Ps. 25:9).

It's hard to trust God if we forget the character of the very One we're afraid to trust. We, on the other hand, forget our helplessness and desire for autonomy. While we may forget, He doesn't. He waits patiently for us to get to the point of emotional exhaustion that leads to our yielding to the One who "will open the heavens, the storehouse of his bounty" (Deut. 28:12). "God is able to do immeasurably more than all we ask or imagine, according to His power that is at work within us" (Eph. 3:20).

Need wisdom? I do. Let's ask God to ready us for it and trust Him in the waiting.

> If any of you lacks wisdom, he should ask God, who gives generously to all without finding fault, and it will be given to him. But when he asks, he must believe and not doubt, because he who doubts is like a wave of the sea, blown and tossed by the wind. That man should not think he will receive anything from the Lord; he is a double-minded man, unstable in all he does.
> —James 1:5–8
>
> You want something but don't get it. You kill and covet, but you cannot have what you want. You quarrel and fight. You do not have, because you do not ask God. When you ask, you do not receive, because you ask with wrong motives, that you may spend what you get on your pleasures.
> —James 4:2–3

Prayer for Wisdom

God, as I seek You, remind me You are near,
Speak truth even if it's not what I want to hear.
What's real in my situation and the sin in me,
When I face it with You, then I'll be set free.
Help me feel the heaviness my chains have made,
Wise in my own eyes, as my agenda I've prayed.
How You want my freedom and anticipate,
My misery to reach its limit, under the weight.

No matter what has happened, or will today,
Empower me to persevere and seek Your way.
As I think upon the times I've sinned before,
You have used hard consequences to shore.
Strengthening my faith, for You will provide,
Encouraging me to stay closer, by Your side.
If not for consequences, I'd be running still,
Refusing Your power, to change me and heal.

My very best is always Your desire for me,
Hem me in close to trust You and just be.
Whatever You command, You always provide,
Enabling the humble to walk when they abide.
Thank You for Your grace that never ever ends,
For loving me enough to discipline me when I sin.
Thank You for Your mercy that never ever ends,
Thank You that You never let my way win.

In the past so many times You have stepped in,
Removing my insanity so I can see my sin.
As You put the brakes on, my heart heard clear,
"No more, My child, this behavior stops here."
Just as You stop the ocean wave, causing it to recede,
You limit the bad consequences if I were to proceed.
Show me again how my perspective is wrong,
Keep drawing my heart to whom I belong.

All wisdom is Yours God, and You answer prayer,
Help me to be willing to follow what You share.
You don't waste Your wisdom, or toss it around,
So may You find my heart fertile, humble ground.
I can't do life without You, You're my only hope,
Change me please to thrive for You, not just to cope.
For You lavish Your love and goodness too,
You deserve a heart sold out and faithful to You.

What wisdom do I need today?

What keeps me from asking?

THIRTY-FIVE

What's Your Number?

Numbers are assigned to us throughout life. They're reflective of how we've been evaluated according to the pattern of this world. Test scores reflect our mental aptitude. Sports ranks and figures reflect our physical ability. Salaries reflect the value that's been placed on our jobs. These and other numbers reflect our success or lack of it, according to the world's standard. Isn't it easy to let these numbers determine our value?

This happened to me. Two numbers, my GPA and ACT scores, became a lens through which I saw myself. Compared to the world's standard, I wasn't smart. Neither number met the requirements for the college I chose to attend, yet I enrolled and the check cleared. I graduated from college with a higher GPA, but that didn't budge my core belief that I was not smart. My worth was still stuck, according to the ways of this world; that is until God obliterated my distorted thinking through a Bible study called Anchored.[6]

The Anchored study teaches every single living person is precious because they're made in the image of the most precious One, God (Gen. 1:27). Preciousness is automatically assigned to every single human, not based on performance but existence. Anchored teaches how to use God's Word to combat lies we've believed.

---

[6] *Anchored: A Bible Study on Self-Worth*, Cindy R. Lee, licensed clinical social worker, 2019.

The study outlines lies the Enemy commonly uses to cripple God's people.

"I'm not smart" is fought by applying Romans 12:2. We are smart when we choose to be mentally alert, see the pattern of this world, and seek God's help to reject it. Mental alertness requires choosing to engage in God's Word and pray so we can "test and approve what God's will is." Being smart is having "a love of learning" (a phrase my friend used when we were doing the study together) in order to engage in His Word. God used this Bible study and my friend's words to release me from the power of these numbers (GPA, 2.9; ACT, 12). God replaced them with the knowledge that I am precious!

Do you know you're precious? Pause and think about it. Do you really know to your core how precious you are, not for what you do, but because you exist? Until we realize this, numbers and this world's standards can hold power over us.

Believers aren't exempt from falling for the world's way of thinking. Do you have a number that you've let determine your value? Does it make you feel less than? If so, ask yourself, "Less than what?" The world's standard, not God's.

In this world, we can't escape the presence of numbers, but we can ask God to release us from the power we give them and let Him show us just how precious we are to Him. Knowing and remembering we are precious frees us from being self-focused. It frees us from the trappings of this world. It frees us to see others from God's perspective and to love others, especially those who don't yet know they're precious.

Power of Numbers

This world assigns us numbers, reflecting what we can do,
We mustn't give them power; they don't determine our value.
Our preciousness is already given, even before our birth,
Being made in God's image, He alone sets our worth.

When we let numbers hold power, we'll feel one of two ways,
Either "less than" or "better than," while inner peace we delay.
The "less than" feel fearful, working hard to measure up,
While the "better than" are too busy judging to see their empty cup.

To keep us busy worrying and judging is the Enemy's plan,
Satan knows man's worth has already been set, by the great I AM.
But for those who don't yet know it, or those who have forgotten,
God not only stamped His imagine on you, but sent His only begotten.

If you've let a number master you, put it in its place,
It isn't your identity, so allow it no more mental space.
You've been purposely planned and fashioned by God's design,
Thank the Lord for who you are, and ask Him to help you align.

When numbers no longer hold us, a new freedom is found,
No longer enslaved by digits, seeing all of us on equal ground.
When remembering each soul encountered has God's imagine too,
It's easier to treat them as precious and love them as Jesus would do.

> Then God said, "Let us make man in our image, in our likeness, and let them rule over the fish of the sea and the birds of the air, over the livestock, over all the earth, and over all the creatures that move along the ground."
> —Genesis 1:26
>
> Whoever sheds the blood of man, by man shall his blood be shed; for in the image of God has God made man.
> —Genesis 9:6

Do I have a number(s) that I've given power?

How does seeing others as made in God's image change how I treat them?

Thirty-Six

In the Silence

It can seem as if God is silent when we pray long and hard for a situation that remains unchanged or deteriorates into an even worse condition. Doubt can crowd out trust that God will answer our prayers. In the silence, God calls us to "consider it pure joy when you face trials of many kinds" (James 1:2). God isn't asking us to be happy about our hard situations but to trust Him to produce a stronger faith because of them (James 1:3).

How do we hold on until our faith grows stronger? We remind ourselves of what is true— God is always working. No matter what our situation looks like, we can fill the silence in the waiting.

God taught me how to fill the silence through my friend, Kelley, during one of my darkest trials. After praying for years for a situation that seemed to worsen with each passing year, I received the call I'd feared. My daughter had attempted suicide and was lying unconscious in the hospital. As hours passed, she began to show signs of brain damage.

Seeing my despair, my friend asked, "Vicky, what are the attributes of God?" My mind was blank at first, but as she began to slowly speak words that describe God, some came to mind and I joined her. God Himself was filling the silence with who He is and forever will be. Nothing had changed in the situation, but God comforted me with

Himself and was strengthening my faith. Miraculously, my daughter awoke with no brain damage, and I'm forever grateful! The trial wasn't over though, the "silence" returned and continued on for years.

Romans 12:12 tells us, "Be joyful in hope, patient in affliction, faithful in prayer." God is our hope and our sure foundation. His Spirit's power will grow our patience as we keep our eyes on who God is, not our situation. As we seek Him in our suffering, we can do as Jesus did, pray in the silence.

On the cross, Jesus experienced real silence as He took on God's wrath due us. When God couldn't be there for Jesus because of our sins, Jesus kept going to His Father. When nailed to the cross, Jesus prayed, "Father, forgive them, for they do not know what they are doing" (Luke 23:34). When the perfect fellowship between Jesus and God was broken, Jesus prayed, "My God, my God, why have you forsaken me?" (Mark 15:34). And before Jesus gave over His spirit and died, He cried out, "Father, into your hands I commit my spirit" (Luke 23:46).

When we can't see God working, may we find comfort in the silence, knowing we're not alone. Throughout Scripture many waited like us, not knowing what was to come.

There were those who lived during the time after the Old Testament had been written and before Jesus came in the flesh. They waited four hundred years for God to speak again.

There were those who watched as Jesus died (Matt. 27:55–56) and as He was placed in the tomb (Luke 23:55).

Silence can be palpable when our circumstances look hopeless. But when truth breaks the silence, hope returns. Our hope is not in the circumstances but in the One present in them. Truth raises our perspective to the eternal One who will never let us go.

When silence overwhelms, read Scripture out loud, listen to a sermon online, play a hymn or worship song and sing along. Ask a fellow believer to speak some of God's character to you, and as some come to mind, join in declaring them. Drown the silence with truth until it fills every crevasse of your soul.

The Comfort of God's Immutability

What comfort God's immutability brings for He cannot change,
Every single one of His character traits are always present and in range.
Provider, Strength, and great High Tower to shield us from the storm,
Comforter, Sustainer, and Securer, holds us together when we're worn.

Whatever traits known of Him are tangible for the soul to hold,
Each one as meditated upon places our mind in the Potter's mold.
They are a sure foundation and never let the trusting down,
Won't erode throughout the ages for they are solid ground.

No trial or depth of struggle is too much for God's traits,
Speak them to your soul and in their presence fear evaporates.
This world is constantly changing, nothing in life stays the same,
Except the traits of God found in His holy Word for us to acclaim.

The grass withers and the flowers fall, but the word of our God stands forever.
—Isaiah 40:8

Yet, O LORD, you are our Father; we are the clay, you are the potter; we are all the work of your hand.
—Isaiah 64:8

I the LORD do not change.
—Malachi 3:6

Jesus Christ is the same yesterday and today and forever.
—Hebrews 13:8

How will I fill the silence of waiting for prayers to be answered?

How does knowing God will never change build my trust in Him?

THIRTY-SEVEN

What Do You Want?

*W*hatever we want for another, even something good, can easily slip into pride.

It's good to want good for another, such as them having a closer relationship with God and a deeper trust in Him.

Christ wanted this for Jerusalem (Luke 13:34). He longed to gather those in Jerusalem like a hen gathers her chicks under her wings, but they weren't willing to be sheltered by Him.

Wanting this isn't the problem. But want not kept in check breeds impatience when we don't receive what we desire.

With perfect patience, Christ didn't try to manipulate those unwilling to accept Him. Instead, Jesus kept His mind set on being "about His Father's business" (Luke 2:49 KJV). Even when the Pharisees told Jesus to leave Jerusalem because Herod wanted to kill Him, Jesus refused to focus on Himself and flee for safety. Instead, He obeyed His Father's will. Jesus knew God's plan for Him was perfect. He told them, "I will drive out demons and heal people today and tomorrow and on the third day I will reach my goal" (Luke 13:32). Then He would leave, because that was what His Father desired. Jerusalem wouldn't see Jesus again until He made His triumphant entry (Luke 13:35).

When we become impatient from not seeing what we want to see happen in others, we either don't realize or have forgotten we don't have control over the situation. We can't make others be the way we think they should be. Impatience not recognized and confessed will lead to words or actions in our attempt to prod others the way we think they should go.

In doing this we have more in common with the other person than we realize. We too need a closer relationship with God. We too need to trust His will, His way, and His timing. In trying to achieve what we want, we're interfering in God's business. We're attempting to assume His position of authority over the lives of others and our own. What we need is a healthy dose of trust in the One whose shoes we're trying to fill.

There's nothing wrong with wanting good—it's what we do with it and which way we direct it. Our want must not master us. We must take it to God and allow it to turn into worship. We need to practice Psalm 37:4, "Delight yourself in the LORD and he will give you the desires of your heart." When our desires are set on Him, our desires will become His desires. It's impossible to delight in the Lord and drift away from Him at the same time. It's impossible to be in awe of Him and seek our own will at the same time.

Granted our delight and awe can be fleeting, but He doesn't grow weary of us. We forget our nature wants to control situations and lives, but God never forgets. God knows we won't be free from our sin nature until we're in heaven. We'll delight in Him, then drift away, and then return to delighting again. The more we intentionally choose to delight, the less time we'll spend drifting. How do we know if we're delighting or drifting? God's desires can bring feelings of longing but never anxiety.

Proverbs 3:5–6 tells us to "Trust in the LORD with all our heart and lean not on your own understanding; in all your ways acknowledge him, and He will make your path straight." We can trust Him with those we love. He, better than us, knows what is best. He, not us, can reach those we long to see changes in, and He can do it in ways we could never imagine.

In the meantime, what changes is He wanting to make in us? Delight in Him, and He'll reveal them.

Desires of the Heart

God gives us our desires when we delight ourselves in Him,
Shows the way out of temptation clear, so as not to sin.
He holds our reputation, causing others to hear and know,
While standing on His promises, His goodness overflows.
We see this especially whenever troubles come our way,
Those who delight in Him aren't carried off in dismay.
No matter the circumstances, when in Him we take delight,
He provides our every need, and gives sleep through the night.

His promise is to give us the desires of our heart,
We'll find His peace more often if we live set apart.
Whenever we delight ourselves in the Lord,
We won't desire what man has but what God has stored.
Those who find happiness in whatever God does,
Trust His heart to give whatever He gives because,
God is only good, so only good can come from Him.
The more we trust His goodness, the less we crave to sin.

Since He is our Maker, He knows us through and through,
As His created we don't have His perfect point of view.
From heaven He sees what is for our very best,
It may come as a blessing, or even through a test.
The test is not for His sake, but for our own,
Tests reveal if our trust for God has grown.
Everything is purposeful, and by perfect design,
Trusting His heart fully, helps our own to align.

The more time we spend in prayer and in His Word,
The more we see our need for Him, the more our faith's matured.
As His way of thinking becomes more often our own,
The more we begin to see a glimpse from His throne.
Leaving us in awe of all He does and doesn't do,
More fully aware of His grace, and His mercy too.
The more we know, the deeper our desire grows,
To want what He desires, our best He alone knows.

Delight yourself in the LORD and he will give you the desires of your heart.

—Psalm 37:4

What do I want in my life?

What do I do with my want?

Thirty-Eight

Beyond Any Expectation

Have you ever expected something to arrive, but when it came you were either disappointed or confused because it was different than you expected? This happened to those living during Christ's first coming and ministry. His coming in the flesh brought excitement in many, such as Mary's aunt Elizabeth (Luke 1:41), the shepherds (Luke 2:8–20), and Simeon and Anna (Luke 2:25–38). But as Jesus began His ministry, excitement waned when he wasn't measuring up to others' expectations of Him. Disappointment became devastation when He hung on the cross.

Can you blame those who were disappointed? Put yourself in their place. From the beginning God had promised One would come, and He would crush the head of the Evil One, Satan (Gen. 3:15). Adam and Eve hung on to God's promise of One to destroy the misery brought on by their sin. The first parents passed down news of the promise, and so did every generation of believers after them. Each generation anticipated the promise, and those giving birth to a boy anticipated all the more because the Promised One was to be male (Isa. 7:14). With each passing generation, the anticipation grew; but so did disappointment.

Then, after thousands of years of waiting, with the last four hundred years absent of revelation from God, the promise was fulfilled.

Mary, a virgin, was given word through Gabriel that the child she bore was the Promised One (Luke 1:26–38). As Jesus took on His ministry, His own family questioned His sanity (Mark 3:21). John the Baptist, having heard confirmation from God Himself, questioned if Jesus was the One. John sent a messenger to ask Jesus, "Are you the one who was to come, or should we expect someone else?" (Luke 7:20).

Jesus had not been as they had expected.

Those of us on this side of the cross know better. We can read and understand what was happening and why. Christ's first arrival is understood, praised without question, and only grows our anticipation for His second coming!

Or does it? Are we falling into the same discouragement of those living during the silent years? Are we giving up on His promised return? When He comes will we be caught off guard?

Before Christ arose, His own didn't know what to expect. We're more like them than we realize. We can read verses of Christ's return and try to imagine it, but nothing can prepare us for what will be seen. We can't fully grasp what His return will be like. He's like no other and does things like no one else. His return won't fall flat. When we see the Creator and risen Savior, it's going to blow us away! When we see Him in all His glory, the One who holds all things together will have to continue to hold us together to keep us from evaporating in His presence (Col. 1:17)!

One thing we can be sure of—His arrival won't disappoint.

The King of All Is Coming Back

The King of all is coming back. What will He find when He returns?
Believers asleep at the wheel or living by faith with expectant yearns?
Will their labor be fueled by love of self or love and gratitude for Him?
Will they be found gratifying their own desires or the Spirit's within?
Discovered feeding upon the world or digesting His spoken Word?
Following the path of the world's famous or by His obedient spurred?

The King of all is coming back. The wait's less today than it's ever been,
Will they be found facing the inner battle with doubt or in faith pressing in?
What'll be found as their compass, looking to self or what's proven true?
Will His return bring regret and sorrow or rejoicing by living anew?
Will a panic be felt as the timer stops or will a relieved sigh be heard?
Will He hear, "Can I have more time?" or "Glory's no longer deferred!"

The King of all is coming back. His own will rise to meet Him in the air.
They now have many questions for Him but then will they even care?
After His own are gone, may His gospel and love linger long in the air,
May those remaining accept truth heard and by faith turn to Him in prayer.
Prophecies fulfilled to remind all what's promised will surely come,
The biggest one anticipated is the return of the King, God's own Son.

But you, man of God, flee from all this, and pursue righteousness, godliness, faith, love endurance and gentleness. Fight the good fight of the faith. Take hold of the eternal life to which you were called when you made your good confession in the presence of many witnesses. In the sight of God, who gives life to everything, and of Christ Jesus, who while testifying before Pontius Pilate made the good confession I charge you to keep this command without spot or blame until the appearing of our Lord Jesus Christ, which God will bring about in his own time—God, the blessed and only Ruler, the King of kings and Lord of lords, who alone is immortal and who lives in unapproachable light, whom no one has seen or can see. To him be honor and might forever. Amen.

—1 Timothy 6:11–16

Therefore God exalted him to the highest place and gave him the name that is above every name, that at the name of Jesus every knee should bow, in heaven and on earth and under the earth, and every tongue confess that Jesus Christ is Lord, to the glory of God the Father.
—Philippians 2:9–11

What are the benefits of expecting God to be who He claims to be?

What are the drawbacks of having expectations of others or myself?

THIRTY-NINE

Training the Unruly

Our sinful nature has the drive and energy of an unruly dog. Before salvation, we were hopeless for anything but sin to master us. It ruled our thoughts and behavior. Through Christ, God has freed us from the mastery of sin's power. Now God is our Master, and He only wants our good. We've been given His powerful Spirit to live within us.

With all this, it's easy to get the idea that living a godly life should be easy, but it's not that simple. Living in this sinful world and with this body of flesh, we still sin. At times we behave like unruly dogs. As believers, we've chosen God as our Master. Only He knows just how to train us and bring about our sanctification. We can't train ourselves any more than an unruly dog can. Only our Master can bring about changes in our heart that leads to permanent changes in our behavior.

No matter how badly we want to be better and how hard we work to improve ourselves, our attempts will likely only be temporary. They may lead to our injury, and that of others, because our thoughts are not His thoughts and our ways not God's (Isa. 55:8).

Our part in the training is to decide and keep deciding who we will trust more, our old master, sin, or our new Master, God. We yield to whomever we trust more at the time.

God is a gentle master. He doesn't force obedience. Until we yield to His mastery, He'll allow us to wander off in the way we're determined to go for a while. While we wander, God waits patiently, knowing our yelp for help is inevitable. God knows all this, and if we're honest with ourselves about our likelihood to wander, so do we. God wants us to turn to Him for help. He doesn't tire of us yelping; He loves to hear His children's call because then they're ready for gentle training.

God uses all the messes we've made in our training. Our wanderings bring empty pleasures. Proverbs 26:11 says, "As a dog returns to its vomit, so a fool repeats his folly." God's language is graphic because the consequences of foolishness are serious. To return to foolishness is to return to the destructive mindset and behavior from which He's freed us.

Before salvation we had no hope, no Spirit indwelling, no power to live differently out of love for the Savior. We had no hope to yield, no hope to change or to act with pure motives.

But now that we are saved, we can embrace our helplessness to train ourselves and look to our faithful Master. He can do for us what we cannot do for ourselves. When we look to God and keep looking, we allow the Spirit to train us. Looking to God is being willing to walk alongside God while He leads.

This might be choosing to spend time reading His Word and talking with Him throughout the day. With an open heart, we learn to recognize His voice over others. We need to know His voice so He can guide us when we've wandered off. In the training, our trust in Him grows. With deepening trust, He grows our patience to wait on the rewards we desire and to accept it more easily when He says not to do some things. In time, our love grows for our Master, as well as a desire to be sensitive to His voice.

Though I've often thought it would be helpful, I have yet to find where our robe of righteousness (Isa. 61:10) comes with a leash. With a jerk of the line, God could inform me of an error. Thankfully He doesn't train like this. If so, I'd become desensitized to it, requiring Him to jerk even harder, leading to whiplash.

Instead, God gives a continual choice before us to choose this day whom we will serve (Josh. 24:15). May His whisper be all it takes whenever we start to wander.

Faithful Master and Teacher

Always the faithful Teacher, God uses all for training,
Shown first to Adam, bringing animals to him for naming.
Seeing every creature, each one God had brought to life,
Adam had no mate as these did, no suitable friend or wife.

Next lesson, to teach His prized creation to trust and obey,
But tragic was the consequence when man chose another way.
The tempter used God's Word, loving guidance mixed with lies,
Now the two were introduced to the masquerader, master of disguise.

Pride replaced peace that day when the two fell for him,
Now full of shame they'd never known, all because of sin.
They tried to cover their own nakedness, hoping for relief,
But God would teach them, only God, could heal their grief.

God came and asked questions, teaching them how to confess,
To learn to acknowledge wrongs done, and to God express.
To see matters of the heart, which brought their sin about,
To learn pain comes from acting upon believed lies and doubt.

Sin never occurs in isolation, it comes with a tribe,
One sin piling upon another, each one fueled by pride.
Soon the two were pointing to another to blame,
Hoping to avoid punishment, brokenness, and shame.

After man's fall into sin, the biggest lesson came to light,
Payment for sin requires death, perfection to cover their plight.
God killed an animal, a limited picture of the Savior to come,
Showing only One could cover the horror of sin, God's only Son.

Adam and Eve understood the lesson, hoping "He" was their first child,
But soon it was made clear to them, the Savior's arrival would take a while.
Now like the first two believers, all look with anticipation for Christ's return,
Until we see Jesus face to face, we like them have many lessons to learn.

> I will instruct you and teach you in the
> way you should go; I will counsel you and
> watch over you.
> —Psalm 32:8

Whose voice do I have a tendency to listen for? My own, another's, or God's?

How have I seen God's faithfulness even when I've failed to listen to Him?

FORTY

Surprise!

Have you ever been given a surprise party? If so, someone went to a lot of work. They carefully strategized the place and time of the event. They contacted your closest friends and family members to gather together for you. If they were successful, you didn't see it coming.

Those in Christ have an even bigger gathering coming, but it shouldn't take us by surprise. It's the day Christ returns for His own. We don't know the time or where we'll be, but we are assured it's happening—He's coming.

We are waiting for the day, so where's the surprise? The ones surprised will be the ones not expecting Him when He comes as promised, like a thief in the night (1 Thess. 5:2).

Why would Jesus be compared to something as scary as a thief? Thieves come in without warning and after they leave, valuables are missing. But this is exactly what will happen when Christ returns to the earth and gathers His church (those who have accepted Jesus as their Savior and Lord). The world hasn't invited Him, but when He comes, His own will be missing (1 Thess. 4:16–17).

Then a deep anguish and confusion will overwhelm much of the world. With us gone, so will be His Holy Spirit. With the Spirit gone, it seems that the world will enter a darkness that is palpable. No one but God has any idea how much work the Spirit is constantly doing through those in which He dwells.

Before Christ's anticipated coming, what are God's own supposed to be doing? The Event Planner has given tasks. He calls us to put on faith and love as a breastplate (Eph. 6:11–14). How do we put on faith and love? We don our armor by being sure of what we hope for and certain of what we do not see every day. We should do this even more when troubles come (Heb. 11:1).

We don the truth that God is a good Father, better than any father we can imagine. He showed His great love by giving His best, His own Son, for His enemies—us.

Lastly, God calls us to put on the hope of salvation as a helmet. Our minds are powerfully destructive, our biggest threat because our depravity is always present. We must bathe our minds with the truth about God, the truth about ourselves, and the truth about Jesus Christ. Let us allow these truths to inspire us to protect our hearts from the sinful things our flesh desires.

We need to preach the gospel to ourselves continually. God is holy, we have no right to ask anything of Him because of our wretchedness, but God chose to give us spiritual life so we will have eternal life with Him. He chose to save us from what we deserve by putting it all on His Son. Why? Because of His great love.

There is no action we do that can earn His gift of salvation. Yet God put His affection on us before we were even created. He delights in us.

Let that seep into your core. If you do, you'll look for Jesus expectantly, anticipating His return.

Until that day, let's love the world boldly. So when we're gone, God's love seen in us will be remembered, missed, and longed for. May the longing draw them to accept what they'd once refused, salvation through Jesus. Then we can be the ones surprised when we see them walk into heaven!

The King Is Coming

The King is coming, the King is coming, He will return some day,
Christ, the King, is who He claims, the Truth, the Life, the Way.

The King is coming, the King is coming, His own trust and believe,
They won't fall for counterfeit signs; the impostor can't deceive.

The King is coming, the King is coming, to rightly take His throne,
When He comes, He'll overthrow one who claims it as his own.

The King is coming, the King is coming, the One who conquered death,
With blazing fire, He'll come from heaven, overthrowing with His breath.

The King is coming, the King is coming, bringing God's children joy!
The impostor sitting upon His earthly throne, His splendor will destroy.

The King is coming, the King is coming, the King is coming for sure,
Hold fast to His teachings, look up often, to find strength to endure.

The King is coming, the King is coming, live to reflect His Light,
Avoid busybodies and the defiant, but welcome back the contrite.

The King is coming, the King is coming, our Savior and our cure,
In the waiting, in the longing, stand firm, love truth, live pure.

The King is coming, the King is coming, the day is closer now,
All will confess His righteousness and every knee will bow.

> God is just: He will pay back trouble to those
> who trouble you and give relief to you who are
> troubled, and to us as well. This will happen
> when the Lord Jesus is revealed from heaven in
> blazing fire with his powerful angels.
> —2 Thessalonians 1:6–7

> Concerning the coming of our Lord Jesus Christ and our being gathered to him, we ask you brothers, not to become easily unsettled or alarmed by some prophecy, report or letter supposed to have come from us, saying that the day of the Lord has already come. Don't let anyone deceive you in any way, for that day will not come until the rebellion occurs and the man of lawlessness is revealed, the man doomed to destruction. He will oppose and will exalt himself over verything that is called God or is worshiped, so that he sets himself up in God's temple, proclaiming himself to be God. . . . And then the lawless one will be revealed, whom the Lord Jesus will overthrow with the breath of his mouth and destroy by the splendor of his coming.
> —2 Thessalonians 2:1–4, 8

Who in my life is also anticipating Christ's return?

Who does God want me to love boldly today?

The Road Well Traveled

The Narrow Road is a messy one, that is from our point of view,
But no mess is too much for our God, always faithful and true.
Paved with grace and mercy, on this road freedom can be found,
As we rest in Him who paved it, we find abundant life profound.

Until we see Christ face to face, let's keep choosing self to sacrifice,
When we do, we'll find as promised, His provision will suffice.
When we set our hearts to who God is and all that He has done,
We'll find our footing, and a deeper desire to walk with His Son.

The road has been well traveled by others in our forever family,
When we reach heaven's shore, we'll see just how large our tree.
Those grafted in from every nation, culture, tongue, race, and tribe,
All worshiping the Savior together, as we then perfectly abide.

Our flesh can make the travel bumpy, but with repentance what a ride,
Growing a deeper love and heart of gratitude for Christ the crucified!
No mess ever threatens God, though the bigger the mess, the deeper our pain,
Yet when our life is on display, God's glorified when we don't live the same.

May we hear, "Well done, good and faithful servant," knowing what that brings,
Rewards of many crowns given by God to lay at the feet of the King of kings.
What earns these words isn't being good, but surrendering to the One who is,
Who chose us before the earth's foundation, and out of great love made us His.

Until heaven may we remember we still need our Savior every day,
Trying to walk the road in our own power only leads our heart astray.
But our Savior never leaves us, and our Guide He never removes,
When looking to Him and not ourselves, His character He only proves.

Even as he chose us in him before the foundation of the world, that we should be holy and blameless before him.
—Ephesians 1:4 ESV

After these things I looked, and behold, a great multitude which no one could count, from every nation and all the tribes, peoples, and languages, standing before the throne and before the Lamb, clothed in white robes, and palm branches were in their hands.
—Revelation 7:9 NASB